A MAN CALLED MAMA

Thanks for your support. May the blessings of God be your source of strength, peace and joy.

Be Encouraged!

Ed Newsome

By Travis Newsome &
Edward J. Newsome

A MAN CALLED MAMA

Authored by Travis Newsome & Edward J. Newsome

Published in the United States of America

Printed in the United States of America

Tea Time Self-Publishing Services

Library of Congress Cataloging-in-Publication Data is available upon request.

ISBN: 9798395306760

Cover Designed by Saqib Mushtaq

Table of Contents

Foreword
Julia V. Johnson

My name is Julia V. McCray Johnson. I have lived in Chappell Hill, Texas all my life-a life that has been rich and fulfilling. I have been to many places, met many people, and seen many things. But there is something special about living in small town Texas. One of the most special things is getting to know people on an intimate and personal level. Being a retired schoolteacher, not much has gone on in the town of Chappell Hill that I do not know about.

I am of an age where I have known all the Newsome children and even had the distinct pleasure teaching six of them in my classroom, as well as having been closely associated with most of the children at the local church. I can truly say that I have never had an ounce of trouble from any of them. I also knew their parents, J.D. ("Mama") and Ina Newsome, very well. "Mama" was my second cousin.

I love the fun, excitement, and even the mystery these children had in writing this book, "A Man Called Mama," because most children just want to go on with their lives without focusing too much on the past; however, this family has done a masterful job of pulling this project together. This book will reveal that everything was not a "bed of roses" for this family; but, at the same time, they have shown that strong family dynamics and solid religious values are tools that can help any family to successfully overcome and embrace any challenges that may arise. Everything has been put on the table.

One unique thing about this book, "A Man Called Mama," is that without knowing what each person has written, the children, and even some of the grandchildren, have each written their separate versions of who they knew their father and grandfather to be. No collaboration among them has taken place. Each will learn what the other has written only when this book is completed and hits bookstores. How interesting and unique! There is a lot we all can learn about life and the challenges it has to offer, to be found in these pages.

Introduction

"A MAN CALLED MAMA"

How could a man called "Mama" have so many children?

Having eleven children, plus an outside kid, the 12th, must have been an easy task, or was it? Regardless, the family grew and grew, and then grew more. How? Who was this man? How did he do what he did? This book will answer your questions about Mama Newsome and may leave you wondering how such a man could do so much with so little. He had no formal education or money, yet he raised each of his children to be prosperous and to impact the nation and the world.

"A Man Called Mama" is a collection of uncollaborative essays written by all of his children and some of his grandchildren. This book is unusual because only one writer knows what the others have written about their father or grandfather. Each writer has written based on their personal experiences, relationships, impressions, influences, and memories of the man called Mama. Each essay will likely be similar in some respects, and very different in many other areas. Be prepared to discover the nuances, and in doing so, to compare each writer's experience to another's experience of life with Mama Newsome.

Everything is laid on the table. No holds barred. There will be some surprises. There will be many questions. There may be some tears and some disagreements, and some disappointments among the authors. There should be no concerns about veracity because each has written based on their own memory and understanding.

One of the book's most exciting aspects should be if and how the siblings address the 'extra' sibling, the brother of another mother (he has his chapter in the book). Everyone says it's "Mama's" baby, but could it be "Papa's"? Maybe! (Papa was the identical twin of Mama). Papa supposedly had no children. Is it possible that Mama and Papa discussed whether or not Papa should claim the baby? They were very close, after all. Mama was married and already had eleven children, the last of whom was born ten years earlier.

This book is written to encourage families to connect and stay connected with one another, no matter the difference, distance, or disposition, because there will always be difficulties, disappointments, and disagreements. Let love and trust be the guiding forces among one another because family is stronger together than apart.

When challenges occur, let them be the very things that pull you back together as a group, and make you even more robust for the journey ahead. After all, blood is thicker than water and love triumphs over hate every day.

This book is written in chronological order by the siblings, and by the grandchildren who chose to contribute their accounts. Robert Sr. was deceased before the writing of this book; however, his story is written by Edward with contributions from the other siblings.

Chapter 1
Robert Lee Newsome

Robert Lee Newsome, Sr. (Posthumously)

This posthumously written story is about Robert Lee Newsome, Sr., and his relationship with "A Man Called Mama", his daddy. Robert died on January 17, 2018, at 80 years old and never had the chance to write his own story about his relationship with his daddy. Therefore, his story is written here by his seven brothers and three sisters. Robert was the firstborn, and we all had an excellent relationship with our parents. While this writing does not include all of Robert's memories, sayings, and experiences relating to our daddy, it attempts to capture as many of those experiences as possible. Based on Robert's conversations over the years, we are exceptionally equipped to write this story as he would have. This story is written in the first person.

I am Robert Lee Newsome, the firstborn child of John Douglas and Ina Turknett Newsome. I was born on May 18, 1937. My parents had a total of 11 children. I was named after one of my uncles. Daddy did not name me after himself because he said he did not believe in naming children "Junior". When I asked him why, he just said that any child should be given his own name, not the name of his father. When I reminded him that not only was my son a "Junior" but also every son he had who had a boy named their sons after them, except for Jerry, and that Travis does not have a middle name but his son Travis' middle name is Alexis, he replied, '*Everyone else can do what the shit they want to do, but not me!*' Daddy insisted that we call him "Daddy", not "Father" because, he said, "There is only one "Father", and that is the Father in Heaven."

To fully appreciate my connection with my dad, I must first tell you something about myself. I was conceived out of wedlock, but my parents married before I was born. As you can already see, my dad had some very colorful language. When I asked Daddy what happened there, he just looked at me, shook his head and said, *'Boy, stop asking me so many shittin' assed questions!'.* I left it at that.

I was the only child in the family until my sister Johnnie Mae was born, 1,249 days, or about three and a half years later. I was delighted to have a little sister. I learned to work very early because I had the task of babysitting my sister at 4.5 years old while my mother was working outside in the garden or the field. Daddy taught me to hold and care for my little sister. Dad's teaching me was one of my earliest memories, in addition to when the Japanese military launched a surprise attack on the United States Naval Base at Pearl Harbor, Hawaii, on December 7, 1941. The next day, December 8, 1941, President Franklin D. Roosevelt asked Congress for and received a declaration of war against Japan. Then, President Roosevelt declared that December 7 was 'A Day of Infamy'. Daddy was only 28 at the time, and my mother was 25.

On September 10, 1940, the United States instituted the Selective Training and Service Act of 1940, which required all men between the ages of 21 and 36 to register with their local draft board. This peacetime conscription was a first for the United States. However, in wartime, all men between 18 and 45 were required to register for the draft and became subject to serve in the military. Daddy, like all men, would have been required to register for the military draft; however, the Selective Service Board made an exception if a man was married and had a child before December 8, 1941. When Dad was reminded of that, he picked me up and said, 'Little rascal, I had you just in time!'. World War II started on September 1, 1939, under President Franklin D. Roosevelt and officially ended on September 2, 1945, under President Harry S. Truman. Later, Daddy told me that he was relieved when World War II was officially over, that he had not had to go off and leave his family.

Being the firstborn, I was given a lot of special attention, probably more than most of my other siblings. My special attention from my parents never ceased, even after the birth of the others. Daddy told me that whenever he knew I was coming home from Kansas City, he'd remind Madear to make sure she set aside some cake or dewberries, especially for me, so the rest of the kids would not take it all before I got home. I was aware that my parents were looking out for me. They did not deny this when my other brothers and sisters brought this to their attention.

My parents were very typical in the sense that we did not have a lot of money (for some strange reason, the perception in the community was that our family had money; maybe we had more land (30.4 acres) than any other Black family in Chappell Hill) but we always had food to eat and clothes to wear; sometimes both the food and clothes were given to us by our family or by people for whom my parents did occasional daywork. Even though we were considered *'poor'*, my daddy never accepted government cheese or commodities for his family.

Dad was a barber. I was unaware of any other Black barbers in Chappell Hill, Texas, the birthplace of my daddy and all my siblings. My Mother was born in the Copling Spring Community, a part of Chappell Hill. In addition to cutting hair, Dad often did farm work in the area, and sometimes Madear did work for some of the white families who lived in our community. Daddy told me he did not like working for someone else and encouraged me to always plan to have something of my own. I kept that in my mind.

My daddy taught me to do manual labor, but, honestly, I was never really skilled at doing manual work. I knew I was not cut out for that kind of work early in life. That did not stop Daddy from trying to teach me to plow the fields, plant the crops, and chop and pick cotton. I started dreaming of other things I could do to make a living and help my parents and family. That is just what kids did back in those days. However, I did not let my daddy onto what I was dreaming because I did not want him to know I did not want to do the manual stuff. I tried to obey and do what he said, but I needed to work faster for his satisfaction. I was doing more dreaming than working. That was the mindset of all my siblings.

My mother enrolled me in C.H. Hogan Elementary School when I was four, and I was placed in a 'pre-primer' class. The school was set up for younger students to go to the pre-primer, then to 'primer' before starting the first grade. The school did not provide lunch, and my parents could only afford two biscuits with butter for my lunch. Even as a 4-year-old, I was embarrassed to take biscuits and butter to school. I envied the other kids with light (white) bread and lunch meat. Then I told Daddy I wanted lunches like the ones the other kids had, and he said, *'Boy, you better be happy with what you got!'.*

We were brought up in church all our lives. Our mother was always a member of the local Methodist church (Saint John African Methodist

Episcopal Church), and Daddy was always a member of the Baptist church (Ebenezer Baptist Church).

Going to church on Sundays was a requirement. I don't recall having ever gone to church with Daddy. I don't remember if there was ever a time when Daddy went to the Methodist church. I don't recall ever missing church on Sunday. The only time Dad ever would've gone to the Methodist church was for a funeral, and then he'd usually sit in the back of the church near the door.

My mother was very active in the church. She sang in the choir, made the sacrament bread for communion, and conducted Easter and Christmas plays, for which all the children had speeches to learn. She did every other duty that needed to be done except to preach. Daddy had no role in his church and never came to any of the Christmas or Easter plays in which we had speaking parts. He was not the 'every Sunday' kind of guy. I loved giving speeches at church and school, but Daddy was never there to hear them.

I always wished he was there but did not ask him to come because I knew he would fuss. Our church conducted a revival once a year, always at night and usually in the summertime, that lasted about two weeks. The revival was usually a more intense worship experience that consisted of singing, praying, and preaching. Another thing that made it different from a regular worship service was the existence of a 'mourners' bench', which was the front seat in the middle of the church. Additionally, it was different because persons (usually young persons) who had not accepted Jesus Christ 'into their hearts' (what is also known as 'getting religion') would take to the mourners' bench and be prayed for and preached over until they had made the decision to invite Jesus into their hearts.

The mourners' bench was only available to children who were 12 years of age or older. Why 12? Twelve was considered to be the "age of accountability" because we were taught that this is the age that Jesus showed some accountability when He stayed behind in the temple and talked to religious leaders after His parents had gone off and left Him. They were not aware that Jesus was not with them until three days later as they walked back to their hometown. His parents turned around and found Him in the temple and scolded Him, and He told His parents that it was time for Him to be about His Father's business. His Father is God. (Luke 2:49).

If the mourner did not reach a point of decision the first year, then they would be expected to return the following year and each year afterwards until they 'got religion'. When a person decides to ask and accept Jesus to come into their heart and believes that Jesus is the Son of God and that Jesus died for their sins and that Jesus rose from the dead, and that Jesus returned to

God in Heaven, then the person is considered saved and has gotten religion. These steps may seem like a lot, but this is what it means to emulate Jesus. I went to the mourners' bench in 1949 at 12 years old. I did not 'get religion' the first year. I had to wait until the following year because there was no other opportunity to get religion. After all, the revival was held one time per year. Neither our parents nor our church teaching believed in just giving the preacher your hand and saying that you wanted to become a church member.

God forbid if you died before the next opportunity to get religion! We were taught that a person who had not accepted Jesus as Lord and Savior would not go to Heaven but would go to Hell! My parents and other religious leaders were staunch believers in this multi-layer process of getting religion to be saved from Hell's fire. I confessed a hope in Jesus Christ on June 8, 1951, at 13. I had made it to the next year without dying! I was happy to get this over with because getting religion was a serious step.

So serious, in fact, that when the church was not in session, the mourner would be expected to seek and pray during the day, all day, usually away from the family, and usually someplace outside, like in the woods, the field, or maybe in the barn, because there was to be no contact with anyone, except when it was time to eat; and, then still no talking to another person, the animals or anything; no playing ball or going to the store to buy candy; nor any other social activity.

This mourning process was complicated for the entire family. Daddy was a firm supporter of this process of getting religion. During the mourning process, I got a break from doing chores. Since the revival was usually held during early summer, by design, there was no cotton to chop and no cotton to pick.

Daddy always taught me the necessity of being sure that I had religion and that I had indeed asked and accepted Jesus in my heart and that I genuinely believed that Jesus died on the cross for my sins, and that I believed that Jesus rose from the dead and is now back in Heaven sitting on the right-hand side of God.

Daddy always said, *'Don't just give the preacher your hand and think you got religion; you must be sure...just giving the preacher your hand and saying you want to join church ain't worth a hill of beans!' In* 1951, just a few months after getting religion, I went off on my first 'cotton pick' with nine other boys to Rosenberg and Needville, Texas, about 65 miles southeast of Chappell Hill and just southwest of Houston. Going on the cotton pick took place in 1951 and 1952. My parents did not go. We would stay from Sunday evening through Friday noon during the cotton pick. I would spend as little money as possible, usually only eating a little, so I could take as much money as possible back home to my parents, usually between $15 or maybe $30 if the rain did not stop us from picking. I just wanted to show Daddy I could be responsible. He was pleased to get whatever money I brought home to support the family.

During the summer of 1953, at 16, Daddy allowed me to go to Houston to work. There, I lived with my cousin, and I worked at the Pepsi-Cola and Golden Age Bottling Company. I often went without food and only drank Pepsi because it was free. Again, whatever money I had left was used to help support my family.

In September 1953, still at 16, my mother's uncle, Julius Williams, came down from Kansas City to visit his sister, Aunt Sue Felder. I asked him if I could return to Kansas City to live with him for the summer.

He told me I could come next summer, but I would have to wait until school was out. Here was my big chance to get out of Chappell Hill and the cotton fields!

I had asked Uncle Julius, but I had not asked my daddy. Daddy was hesitant because he had plans for me to go back to Houston or Rosenberg to pick cotton. Neither he nor my mother were too excited about having their firstborn living so far away from home. What would I do there? Where would I live? How would Uncle Julius treat me? How are the people there? I would have no other place to go if things did not turn out well with Uncle Julius, an uncle whom I had never met before.

After two days, Daddy gave me the green light and told me I could go. On May 12, 1954, after school was out, I left Texas and went to Kansas City, Missouri, by bus, supposedly for the summer. Daddy purchased my bus ticket. Once in Kansas City, with Uncle Julius' help, I got a job working on an ice truck, delivering ice to homes in the communities, hollering, *'Ice man! Ice man! Get your ice!'.* The ice was chiseled into cubes about 18 inches square. Many homes didn't have refrigerators then, so the customer put the ice in an icebox or a large bucket. I was getting the hang of things in Kansas City, so I wrote and asked my parents if I could stay in Kansas City after the summer. Daddy was still hesitant because he thought I would return home to Chappell Hill after the summer.

Reluctantly, he allowed me to stay, but not before giving me fatherly advice in a letter, saying: *'Son, make sure you watch yourself. Don't take wooden nickels; Be careful how you talk to people and don't be up there sassing people out. Do you understand? Make sure you write to us and let us know how you're doing.'* In my following letter, I assured Daddy I would heed his advice and write often. I could feel some reluctance in every word Daddy wrote.

Did he really think he had raised me to take care of myself? Was he really worried about me without saying so? Was he really missing his firstborn but not saying so?

After getting clearance from my parents to stay in Kansas City, I enrolled in Manual High School, 1215 Truman Road, near where I lived with Uncle Julius.

I tried to enroll as an 11th grader, but school officials put me in the 10th grade because I had only completed the 9th grade before I left Texas. I still lived with and worked for my uncle, who owned some apartment buildings.

In addition to attending school, I had taken up a trade- painting and sign painting. My work consisted of cleaning the apartment buildings owned by my uncle, turning on/off the heat and lights, and doing whatever was necessary. To me, this was better than picking cotton!

I would get up at 6:00 AM, and work until 8:05 am, when it was time to go to school. As promised, I wrote back home to my parents to let them know what I was doing. Daddy usually did not write back, but my mother often reported that Daddy was doing okay and finally said he was proud of me. That made me feel good because

Daddy had never said those words to me before to my face.

Daddy was never really too expressive. He never said, *'I love you, son.'* He always said, *'I love all of you!'* It was just who he was, and I had to live with that. Nevertheless, I knew he cared and hoped for the best for all his children and me.

Daddy was proud of me, but maybe I was not doing as well as he thought I was doing. Sometimes I did not have the proper clothes to wear to school. I took a second job working at night to make more money and to get away from Uncle Julius because he was very mean to me, even striking me at times. He made me feel as if I could do nothing right. I didn't tell my daddy this because he would have wanted me to come back home to Texas. On May 11, 1955, one day short of a year of living with Uncle Julius, I told him I was moving out of his place and going to move in with my friend. I knew he would not allow me to leave, so I went to the police station and informed them of the circumstances and my plans. I had found a better job making $26 per week.

They told me that when I got ready to move to let them know, and they would send a police car. When the police came into the house, my uncle said he would let me go, but rather than letting me go to live with a friend, I would have to move back to Texas with my parents. Not wanting to cause trouble with my uncle, I followed his demand, caught a Greyhound bus, and returned to Texas. I shared with my dad how my uncle had been to me. My dad was extremely upset with how my uncle treated me. He considered returning to Kansas City to settle the score with my uncle, but I told him it was not worth it.

After being in Texas for almost a week, I told my parents I wanted to return to Kansas City because I had a friend with whom I could live. Daddy was unsure because he thought my uncle would track me down and start more trouble for me.

On May 17, 1955, I returned to Kansas City with only one nickel in my pocket. My friend told me I could not stay with him because I needed to pay him $2 in advance. I started walking and praying just as my mother had taught me to do when I needed to get divine help. I walked to a transient hotel, and the attendant, Mr. Johnson, whom I had never met, told me I could stay at the hotel but needed $4 in advance. When I told him I had no money, he said, *'Son, your face looks good, but I can't put it in the cash register.'* Then, suddenly, it appeared as if something hit Mr. Johnson, and it seemed like he jumped and then said, *'I have a vacancy in Room 201.'* (Obviously, he had been touched by the Lord).

The next morning, the maid knocked on the door and offered me an egg, but I told her, *'No, thanks!'* because I knew I would return to my job three days later. I was without food from

Saturday to Tuesday. For some strange reason, all the advice my daddy had given me flashed in my head, and suddenly I was not hungry.

Daddy had his ways. But he was a sage—a wise man. Daddy was a proud man. He never wanted anyone to know his business. I remember one morning we went to pick cotton for a Polish farmer whose farm was a few miles from our home. Madear always ensured we had something to eat before going to the field.

On this particular morning, she had made enough chicken for us to have a piece and some biscuits for us to take. Because she did not have enough ingredients to make the biscuits thick to her liking, they were made much thinner than usual. As fate would have it, when we got to the field, we discovered that we had lost the biscuits somewhere on the road. Daddy got overly concerned and instructed me to get on Old Filly, our horse, and ride her as hard and fast as possible to find the lost bread. Daddy's main concern was finding the thin hard bread before his aunt Maggie, who generally walks that road, came along the road, and found the bread. He knew if she saw the biscuits, she would go back to town and tell everyone how pitiful the bread was, thus possibly embarrassing Daddy because he was too poor to afford decent bread for his family.

Sure enough, I got on Old Filly and rode her as hard and fast as she could go. I found the biscuits along the road before Aunt Maggie or anyone else could get to them and brought them back to the field where Daddy and the others were anxiously awaiting.

Even though the biscuits were thin, this was some of the best bread we had ever had.

In July of 1955, I started dating Wilma Gates, a lady I had met while delivering ice. She was living with her parents. We fell in love and decided to get married. When we decided, I did not want to write and tell my parents I was getting married, so I caught a bus and went back to Texas to tell them about the news in person. It was out of respect for my parents; after all, I was the firstborn and wanted to make sure they were okay with my decision. Before I left Kansas City, I knew I would not have enough money to return, but I felt I had made the right decision. Actually, I did not have enough money to buy anything to eat while on the bus. A lady was eating cheese, crackers, and salami and offered to share some of it with me. I reluctantly accepted and arrived home in Texas without feeling too hungry.

My parents were happy with my decision to get married, and Daddy thanked me for coming so far to tell them the news. He said, *'Son, you must be doing okay to come here. You could have written us a letter.'* I responded, *'Daddy, truthfully, I don't have my fare to return to Kansas City, but I just wanted to share the news with you and*

Madear in person.' The glad look on their faces from the news I shared suddenly turned into silent questions*: 'What are your plans? How do you plan to get back? What will you do?'* I knew they didn't have the money to help me return to Kansas City.

Before they said anything or offered any suggestion, I answered their many silent unasked questions: 'Don't *worry, I will stay a week and pick some cotton to make enough money to get back home. I will be okay!'* That is what I did; I picked cotton and got the money I needed.

I had a great time with my family and never regretted for one minute the decision I made. I was still living in the transient hotel where the maid offered me the egg when Wilma and I married on September 25th, 1955.

Yes, Daddy came to my wedding along with my mother and my oldest sister, Johnnie Mae. I was extremely pleased that they made such a sacrifice for me. I felt exceptional and honored that they had driven so far to be at my wedding. Our cousin Sandy Newsome helped with the driving. Daddy asked Sterling, who was 13 years old, to stay and watch the other children: Joe, Edward, Joyce, Travis, Jerry, and John. Delores and Oscar were not yet born. Not able to afford our own place, we stayed with Wilma's mother for a month until we got our own place in the same apartment building where Wilma's mother was living. I didn't return to school that fall of 1955. After all, I needed to find a better job because now, I had rent and utilities to pay.

On May 2nd, 1956, I got another job making $1 per hour. On September 7th, 1956, Wilma gave birth to our son, Robert, Jr.

In the spring of 1957, I took my family back to Texas to meet my parents and my family. This time I had enough money to travel.

For another three and a half years, I did not go home again until December of 1960. On this trip, I found out that Sterling, the 3rd child of my parents, had started drinking, smoking, gambling, and had quit school. I told Daddy I wanted Sterling to come to Kansas City so I could help him get himself together. I told Sterling he could come to live in Kansas City with me, but he had to promise to stop drinking and smoking and return to school. Daddy felt that Sterling, who by then was 18 years old, was out of control and he agreed that going to Kansas City would be a good thing for him since he could not tell him anything or do anything with him.

After working for one month and a half, I earned enough money to buy Sterling a bus ticket to Kansas City. He arrived in Kansas City, without a topcoat, on a freezing day, January 20th, 1961, the same day that President John F. Kennedy was inaugurated. I had also quit school just before I got married, but I returned to night school and earned enough credits in 1961 to obtain my high school diploma.

From the very beginning, our family has always been close. Daddy was relieved and thanked me for saving Sterling's life. I just saw it as a way of helping him to get a new start in life. Daddy and Mother had always encouraged us to do what we could for each other. Since I was the oldest, they expected me to take the lead in helping my younger siblings. Sterling stopped smoking on March 4th of 1961, after he attended a healing revival where the preacher laid his hand on Sterling and healed him. The preacher did not heal Sterling from drinking, but Sterling did stop drinking a short time later. Another bad habit that Sterling had was cussing. He could out-curse a sailor.

When Sterling attended the revival, his drinking and cussing were not 'on the table', only smoking. He decided on his own to put those other two habits down. I was proud of him, and I informed Daddy of Sterling's changes. Daddy could only say, *'Thank you, Jesus!'* but that was enough.

Sterling was in Kansas City a few months before Joe arrived in June of 1961. It was easier for Daddy to let Joe leave home to come to Kansas City because of Sterling's success.

Daddy was sad that his boys were leaving home, one by one, but he was happy that they would have a chance to get better jobs and do something productive with their lives. Eventually, most of my siblings would follow in my footsteps and move to Kansas City. After Sterling and Joe, the succession went like this:

· Edward- July 18, 1963 (after he and Ma' dear left a church convention in St. Louis)
· Travis- June 7, 1973 (after graduating from the University of Oklahoma)
· Delores- June 17, 1973 (after high school and Father's Day)
· Jerry- August 21, 1973 (after attending Blinn Junior College in Brenham, Texas. Oscar came to help him drive)
· John- August 10, 1975 (after getting out of the U.S. Navy)
· Oscar- November 20, 1984 (after getting out of the U.S. Army)
· Joyce lived in Kansas City from the fall of 1955 to the spring of 1956 and attended school for one year before going back home)
· Johnnie spent the summer of 1958 with me in Kansas City; Jerry came with her.
· My mother never stayed but visited Kansas City frequently.
· Daddy never stayed, but came for several weddings: mine, Edward's, Travis', Jerry's, and Delores'

· Johnnie Mae and Joyce had visited me in Kansas City, but both stayed briefly. I am sure Daddy did not encourage the young ladies to stay in Kansas City because he had apprehension, even about the boys staying so far away from home.

Having many of my siblings in the city with me was like having heaven on earth. I was always so proud of them for not getting into trouble and for being so close to me.

We had great times and did many things together, working and playing. More than anything else, this brought so much joy and excitement to Daddy and Madear to have all of us working and doing things together. Joyce and Johnnie Mae probably felt a greater need to stay closer to our parents to help care for them in times of need. Daddy was always so proud of us and walked and talked with pride when he spoke to others about his children. It was always good to see his reaction to us coming home to visit, when he was around other people. It was also always good to come back home to Texas and receive all the special treatment from Daddy and Madear.

Even after we all got older, our parents treated me a little differently from the other children by having the particular kinds of food they knew I liked. They always wanted to hear *'what Robert Lee'* thought or said about things. When they called or talked with any other siblings, they always asked, *'How is Robert Lee doing?'* Once, Joyce told me that Daddy said, *'Robert Lee's got more sense than all y'all put together!'*

I disagreed; but maybe he had this bloated feeling about me because I was his *firstborn.*

One of Daddy's favorite sayings about a person who was trying to be all that 'and a bag of chips,' was, *"Ahh, he thinks he's a bigshot! Look at him, trying to be big, but little is eating his ass up!'* On a visit to Kansas City in 1979, my mother and I went to a political rally for city Councilman Bruce R. Watkins, who was running for Mayor of Kansas City. When Daddy saw pictures of us flanking the candidate, he replied*, 'Ahh shuckie now, y'all be some bigshots!'* He did not add the other part that generally follows that descriptive phrase. On another occasion, when Mother was in town in 1984, I took her to another political rally for former Minnesota Senator and former Vice President Walter Mondale. When Daddy saw the pictures we took with him, again, he referred to us as *bigshots*. He felt proud that I was taking Madear to different places, but he felt prouder because he saw me involved and connecting with influential people.

But as for himself, he said that he *'could give a dog's ass'* to be hanging around such people. Daddy was not into politics much, but he kept abreast of a few national things. He actually voted for President Richard M. Nixon instead of John F. Kennedy in the 1960 presidential election. He said that since he had to pay a poll tax before he could vote, then, '*I will vote for any damn person I want to, and that's final. Shit on what people think about me!*'

I had a chance to meet former President Bill Clinton in his first term of office. I told Daddy about my meeting and my brief visit with the President, and all he said was, *'Un huh, that's good,'* and went on about his business. I never bothered to tell him about me taking Madear to hear a speech given by Bishop Desmond Mpilo Tutu (South African Bishop and anti-apartheid and human rights activist) when he was speaking in Kansas City at the University of Missouri-Kansas City in the early '90s. I don't know if Madear remembered to mention it to him. But, knowing how Daddy talked, I can only imagine what he would have said.

Daddy was not present at many of the events in my life. He attended my wedding and a couple more of my siblings' weddings. However, Daddy always showed deep concern for the things that were going on for all of us. But he was not the kind of man who would, or could, jump on a train, plane, or bus at the *'drop of a hat.'* Nevertheless, I knew that he always cared and prayed for his children.

On July 24, 1955, an incident happened to me at my high school when I was hit in the head and almost drowned during a swimming class. Before losing consciousness, I remember crying, *'Lord, save me!' I knew* my Daddy prayed for me in this manner every day; Even though he was not there, I always felt his prayers for me.

In April 1987, I provided a business acquaintance with some professional advice on purchasing a piece of real estate. He lost money due to poor management and demanded that I reimburse him for his losses. When I refused, he became furious and put out a contract on my life to have me killed. In an attempt to fulfill the contract, I was shot four times with a 38-caliber pistol, at close range, on June 8, 1988, in the parking lot of my office building. As the first shot rang out, I had the presence of mind to pray, just as my Daddy had taught me to do when I was in danger or trouble. I prayed, *'Lord, help me!'* As more shots hit my body, I continued to pray: *'Lord, have mercy on me! Lord, save me!'* I never had any doubt my prayers would be answered because after all, the Lord had saved me on June 8, 1951, when I accepted him as my Savior. Thank God for answering my prayers! While I recovered in the hospital for two weeks, my wife and siblings were at my bedside day and night. My siblings were armed just in case I needed extra protection. I had to convince Daddy that everything was going okay and that he did not need to come to Kansas

City for anything. I reminded him that the Lord had already saved my soul on June 8th, 1951, and that he had now saved my life on the same day 37 years later.

The person responsible for the shooting was convicted, got two life terms, and is still serving time in prison. The person who actually pulled the trigger got a four-year sentence in state prison. While in prison, he called me often and asked me to help him get out. He said he was ready to start going to church and turn his life around. I mentioned this in a conversation with Daddy, and Daddy said, *'No, let his chicken-shit ass stay right there in jail where he belongs. I hope his ass rots in there!'*

Believing that my assailant was sincere, I went against Daddy's advice, and I wrote a letter to the parole board and told the board that I did not object to him being released. I met with the shooter after he was released from prison and said to him that I forgave him and that I loved him, and that I was willing to help him pull his life back together; however, he did not allow me to help him; he got into more trouble with the law; and not wanting to go back to prison, he committed suicide. I knew Daddy would not have been as lenient as I was, nor would many other people have been as forgiving if someone had tried to take their life. This ordeal was challenging for my family, but we stuck together, prayed for one another, and took whatever measures were necessary to protect our family.

My daddy and my siblings were proud of me and always did everything they could to help me. Several of us siblings were in business together, and we often did business ventures.

Daddy had always taught me to be a leader. He told me to set the right example because my siblings would always watch me and want to do what I did. When we were kids, my sister Johnnie Mae once tried to follow me under the schoolhouse. Other than playing, I am trying to remember why I went under the schoolhouse.

I have already talked about them coming to Kansas City. When I started the real estate business, several brothers joined me in the industry. I grew up as a Methodist but changed my denomination to Baptist because my first wife was Baptist. My siblings also grew up in the Methodist church but changed to Baptist when they moved to Kansas City. Johnnie did not move to Kansas City but converted to Baptist many years ago while living in Houston.

I never wanted to disappoint or embarrass my parents, especially my daddy. Even as an adult, I wanted them to be proud of me. In the summer of 1962, I purchased a beige 4-door 1949 Studebaker for $40. Sterling, Joe, and I drove the old car home to Texas.

We had a flat tire, and when we stopped to fix the tire, it abruptly stopped raining. I vividly remember it rained very hard from Kansas City to Waco, Texas, some 635 miles. The old car, funny-looking and tattered, and with an extra spare tire tied on the top, got us where we needed to go. Because of how the old car looked, I was too ashamed and embarrassed to drive it to Daddy's house, and I decided I wanted to leave the vehicle in Brenham, some 10 miles away. But Sterling convinced me to drive the car home because leaving it somewhere after it had brought us this far was silly. We wheeled the Studebaker into the front yard close to the front door of my parents' little bungalow.

Daddy came outside to greet us, looked at the Studebaker, withheld his infectious laugh, and said, *'Thank God y'all made it safely!'* He could care less about how the old Studie looked. He was delighted to see his three oldest sons come home. Even with his *crassness* and *gruffness*, he had a way of settling down any nervousness about the old Studebaker. That's the kind of daddy he was.

My daddy was not perfect, nor did he profess to be. As far as those matters, we are all flawed. God knows that I am not perfect. Sometime after 1970, he shared with me that he had been *carrying on* with another woman, which resulted in the birth of a boy child, born in August of 1969, almost ten years after the birth of his youngest son, Oscar. Daddy did not seek my forgiveness for his action, nor did I request anything from him. Whatever he needed to do about the matter was between him and his God. I stood by my daddy as he shared his heart with me. Needless to say, I was shocked, surprised, and saddened. He was very contrite and was accepting of his transgressions. He was also accepting of his responsibility to his baby. He did not ask me to keep this information from my siblings or tell me not to tell my mother. He trusted my heart. Daddy did not share this information with any of his other children.

After a time had passed, I shared the information with some of my siblings living in Kansas City. By now, my other siblings who were living in Texas had already gotten wind of what had taken place. I am unsure how much time passed before Daddy told my mother, but he did tell her. Dealing with this matter was certainly not an easy task, but my parents found a way to move forward with their lives together.

Daddy and I had occasional conversations about his ninth son. He indicated that he was doing his best to provide for the baby. I listened, but I did not offer much advice. He did not ask for my advice.

I got a chance to meet my half-brother several years after he was born. I even had the opportunity to visit him at his mother's home in Chappell Hill. Daddy encouraged me to develop a relationship with the boy. I always gave the child a small amount of money when I saw him. To me, there was no question whether the boy was my daddy's child. Later on, as the child grew in stature, it was plain to see that he had the looks, the laugh, and many of the mannerisms of my daddy, more so than I or any of my other siblings, especially my brothers. After more years had passed, all my other siblings had a chance to meet their half-brother. He had some reservations about meeting them, and they had reservations about meeting him. The meeting was slightly awkward, but by the time it was finished, there was laughter and hugging, and plans to get together again were made.

In later years, my daddy started experiencing some health issues. At this point, he had never made mention of this son to anyone else except me.

He was aware that all of his children knew one another to some degree, but still, he never said a word to the ten others. On one of my visits to see my daddy when he was ill, he pulled me aside and asked me to make sure that the boy had a suit to wear to his funeral. I promised him that I would.

I was in Arkansas when I learned Daddy had gotten sick. Johnnie told Daddy that I was on my way. In other words, hold on. Being Daddy's favorite, I am convinced he held on to say good-bye to me. I was so happy to get to see him onc last time. My daddy, "A Man Called Mama," passed away at a hospital in Brenham, Texas, on November 13th, 1995, with me, my mother, and my three sisters, Johnnie Mae, Joyce Marie, and Delores Faye, at his bedside. All of his children attended Daddy's funeral, including his youngest son.

When I was much younger, I was well-known for making long speeches. I would walk up and down the dirt road practicing and acting out my speeches.

One big speech I performed was called, 'A Negro in it!', a very long speech posted here. I performed this speech for a school closing as a young boy when I attended C. H. Hogan School. Some of the school officials did not want me to give the speech because of the racial overtones, but with solid support from my daddy and mother, I performed the speech anyway. Daddy did not mind challenging authority when he felt he was in the right, especially when it came to his children. I loved him for that.

"A Negro In It"
By Lena Mason

In the last civil war,
The white folks, they began it,
but before it could close
The Negro had to be in it.

At the battle of San Juan hill,
The rough-riders they began it;
But before victory could be won
The Negro had to be in it.

The Negro shot the Spaniard from the tree,
And never did regret it;
The rough-riders would have been dead to-day
Had the Negro not been in it.

To Buffalo, McKinley went,
To welcome people in it;
The prayer was prayed, the speech made,
The Negro, he was in it.

September sixth, in Music Hall,
With thousands, thousands in it,
McKinley fell, from the assassin's ball,
And the Negro, he got in it.

He knocked the murderer to the floor,
He struck his nose, the blood did flow;
He held him fast, all nearby saw,
When for the right, the Negro in it.

J. B. Parker is his name,
He from the state of Georgia came.
He worked in Buffalo, for his bread,
And there he saw McKinley dead.

They bought his clothes for souvenirs,
And may they ever tell it,
That when the President was shot,

A brave Negro was in it.

He saved him from the third ball,
That would have taken life with it,
He held the foreigner fast and tight,
The Negro sure was in it.

McKinley now in Heaven rests,
Where he will ne'er regret it,
And well he knows, that in all his joys,
There was a Negro in it.

White man, stop lynching and burning,
The black race, trying to thin it,
For if you go to Heaven or Hell
You will find some Negroes in it.

Parker knocked the assassin down,
And beat him, he began it.
In order to save the President's life,
Yes, the Negro truly was in it.

You may try to shut the Negro out,
The courts, they have begun it,
But when we meet at the judgment bar
God will tell the Negro is in it.

Pay them to swear a lie in court.
Both whites and blacks will do it,
Truth will shine, to the end of time
And you will find the Negro in it.

There was another speech I loved so much that I used to perform. It is called "Somebody's Mother" – Written by Mary Dow Brine.
This poem touched my heart more than anything because it made me think about my mother and grandmother. My daddy always taught me to be unselfish, help others, have compassion and kindness, and think of others more than myself. Daddy helped many people even when he did not have much himself. This powerful principle that I learned from him helped guide my life.

"Somebody's Mother"
- Mary Dow Brine (1816-1913)

The woman was old and ragged and gray,
And bent with the chill of the Winter's Day.

The street was wet with a recent snow,
And the woman's feet were aged and slow.

She stood at the crossing and waited long,
Alone, uncared for, amid the throng.

Of human beings who passed her by
Nor needed the glance of her anxious eyes.

Down the street, with laughter and shout,
Glad in the freedom of "school let out."

Came the boys like a flock of sheep,
Hailing the snow piled white and deep.

Past the woman so old and gray
Hastened the children on their way.

Nor offered a helping hand to her –
So meek, so timid, afraid to stir.

Lest the carriage wheels or the horses' feet
Should crowd her down in the slippery street.

At last came one of the merry troops
The gayest laddie of all the group.

He paused beside her and whispered low,
"I'll help you cross, if you wish to go."

Her aged hand on his strong young arm
She placed, and so, without hurt or harm.

He guided the trembling feet along,
Proud that his own were firm and strong.

Then back again to his friends he went,
His young heart happy and well content.

"She's somebody's Mother, boys, you know,
For all she's aged and poor and slow.

"And I hope some fellow will lend a hand
To help my mother, you understand,

"If ever she's poor and old and gray,
When her own dear boy is far away."

And "somebody's mother" bowed low her head
In her home that night, and the prayer she said
Was "God be kind to the noble boy,
Who is somebody's son, and pride and joy!"

CHAPTER 2
Johnnie M. Newsome-Lewis

Our dad was a man called Mama. He had an identical twin brother, called Papa. You get it? Mama and Papa? Our dad was the younger twin. His given name was John Douglass. John Douglass has always been spelled Douglas with one 's', but on his birth certificate it's spelled Douglass J.D. His twin brother's given name was James Columbus, J. C. Uncle J.C. did not have any children. They had two older brothers. The oldest had six children, and the second oldest had one son. I never found out why Mama Lottie-our grandmother, whose name was Lottie Mays, and Daddy Bud-our grandfather, whose name was Phillip Newsome, decided to give them such odd nicknames.

I understand that when they were younger, they would get into trouble, pulling tricks on their mother, and all sorts of things, and as a result both would get whippings. Sometimes one would get a whipping for the other because Mama Lottie didn't know which one was being naughty.

They grew up on a farm, having to work in the cotton and corn fields, feeding the hogs, (or as they called it, slopping the hogs,) and milking the cows.

Then there were chickens, ducks, and geese to be fed, and all sorts of other chores to do. They raised their chickens just as they did many other things. My dad spoke of the time when Mama Lottie had them kill a chicken, which involved wringing the head off, and throwing the chicken under one of those big #3 tubs so it couldn't flop all over the yard in the dirt and grass. After that, they'd have to scald the chicken in hot water to remove its feathers. When they had finished scalding the chicken, they started on the inside removing and discarding stuff. When they got to the chicken gizzard, they cleaned and pulled away everything that they could.

They were so excited to please their mother. They would take the gizzard inside and say, "See Sa' Lottie, we threw all of that ole yellow stuff away", thinking that was the right thing to do. But Mama Lottie would say, "Oh no that was the good fat, and I wanted to keep that". They did not get fussed at, though, because they thought that was the thing to do. They never called her mother or Mama. Sa' Lottie was short for Sister Lottie.

Daddy, a man called Mama, and his three brothers were hard workers, because they had hard working parents. Their mother was a very strong disciplinarian. She wanted to make sure they had their own farm and a place to live, so she purchased 30.4 acres of land around 1934. After running into a little hardship, our grandmother moved to Fort Worth, TX to work as a live-in maid to help pay for that farm.

Daddy attended C.H. Hogan Jr. School, where he met our mother, Ina Turknett after she moved to Chappell Hill, from the Copling Spring, Texas community.

As An Adult

Daddy and Madear were married in 1937. They lived in Daddy's Grandma Carrie's house until it caught on fire and burned down. After that, they lived on the farm that our grandparents had purchased. He continued to work on the farm and provide for his family just as he had been taught by his parents. They had their first son in 1937, and as the years passed their family increased.

While living on the farm, Daddy had his own horses and mules to help in the fields to provide for his family just as his parents had done. He had his own garden and planted cotton and corn. He raised pigs, hogs, and cows. I can remember when we got older, he also had us working in the fields, especially my brothers. They had to help pick cotton, pull corn, feed the animals, milk the cows, and slop (feed) the hogs. They had to make a trough from wood to put the food in for the hogs. Once the pigs had grown enough to turn into hogs, some would be sold for extra income, and some would be slaughtered to provide food for the family. We would always look forward to when the time came to kill a hog or hogs, because it meant that we would have plenty of good fresh pork, sausage, and bacon for a long time. Cooking out the meat with the skin served many purposes. Daddy made lard that we'd use for frying food. The skin part was dried out and used to make crackling to eat or to cook crackling bread (cornbread). No part of the hog was wasted. The small intestines were used as casings for the sausage, and the large intestines (chitterlings) were also eaten.

There were other means of provision, which added to our income such as picking dewberries and pecans. We'd sell some dewberries, and keep some to make desserts. The pecans we'd pick were collected from someone else's property, so we'd have to divide them 50/50 with the landowner so he could sell his half. Daddy and my brothers would go out into the pastures and hunt for wild game, such as rabbits and squirrels. Daddy was a cook also. He cooked rabbit and gravy, and some of his favorite dishes to cook were sweet tomatoes, and rice pudding. Many years ago, he cooked tea cakes one time. Tea cakes were Madear's specialty. Daddy was very proud of his tea cakes, and he wanted us to say they were better or as good as hers, but the truth is, they were not. He enjoyed getting in the kitchen once in a while, because I think he had fun impressing us.

Even when harvest season was over, Daddy still had means of providing for his family, because he was also a barber. He had a shop previously owned by his uncle who had been a barber in downtown Chappell Hill. Even though there was another barber in Chappell Hill named Willie Williams, known as Fat Jack, Daddy had the majority of the customers who were local residents.

I've never seen my dad, or his twin brother wear a shirt that wasn't white. Our dad worked in the fields, and yes, he wore his white shirts even in the fields. If he ever wore any other kind of shirt, it was one that had been given to him. Another strange thing about him wearing white shirts, is that they were always long sleeved and never buttoned down at the wrist unless he was going to church. He wore them with the cuff folded back to his forearms. He wore suspenders with old dress pants to the field. I don't remember if he wore khakis, but he never wore blue jeans. He did sometimes wear overalls.

Our dad was an early riser. Most of the time he would get out of bed at 4 or 5 o'clock in the morning and sit in his recliner with his snuff or tobacco. Daddy never stayed in bed after sunrise. One morning Madear noticed he was still in bed later than usual, so she decided to keep quiet, by tiptoeing around the house being careful not to make noise that would wake him up. Yet, Daddy still managed to wake up and get up before the sun had risen. He asked Madear why she didn't wake him up. She replied "I wanted the sun to catch you in bed for once". He did not believe in staying in bed late. He believed that was a sign of laziness.

He had such an impact on my life. I am an early riser to this day. I can still hear his voice saying, "It's time to get up!"

He was not a coffee drinker, though he loved the smell of coffee. Sometimes he would get up and eat cereal, but not with milk, because he didn't like it. Even though we had cows to milk, he would mix his cereal with orange juice. His twin brother lived with them for a while. They got along very well together, even though both talked like they were fussing most of the time. They really were not fussing. Daddy tried to act like he was the big bad wolf, but he wasn't. He was kind. He did a very good job taking care of his family, to the point that outsiders thought we were rich, and would wonder how Mama took care of all of us children. Many times, he would tell us about saving money. He would always say, "If you make a dollar, you ought to save a quarter".

Emotional

Everyone thought of Daddy as being harsh. There were times he could become emotional. The first time I saw Daddy become emotional was in the 1950's when our first cousin Corine Newsome-Matthew had some issues and had to be admitted to a mental hospital. She was back and forth in the hospital. One time after the ambulance had picked her up and was leaving Daddy had to open the gate for them. He said in his crying voice "I just don't know what's wrong with that poor girl". Even though I was very young, I will never forget the sadness on my daddy's face at that time.

Living Conditions

In the 1950's, before my daddy and some of my brothers built our parents a new home, our old house was not in very good condition. During the storms we had to cover the windows and mirrors, then sit in the corners and be very quiet. We were not allowed to say a word. I am not sure why the mirrors were covered.

When there was a hurricane in the forecast, Daddy would always wait a while to see if the weather was going to get bad, and most of the time it did. Daddy would call all of us together to make sure we were in one room. We would cover all the mirrors and windows and sit in a corner. Daddy would call our names one-by-one to make sure we were all accounted for. Often, we had to grab our things and run up to our grandmother's house, which was in the pasture about two city blocks away. We had to run as fast as possible, sometimes falling down in the dark with the lightning being our only source of light. We would stay until it was all over or until the next morning.

A Christian Man

I can remember Daddy teaching us and telling us about Jesus early in life. He taught us about getting saved or being saved. During the old times they called it 'getting religion'. Getting religion meant getting on the mourner's bench (the front pews), or the front seat in the church during revival time, which was every summer. He would not let us get on the mourner's bench until we were 12 years old, because that was the age of Jesus when He went about His Father's business (Luke 2:49). He made sure we had gotten religion, and accepted Jesus as our personal Savior before we got up and joined the church or had given the preacher our hand. Many of us had to go back to the mourner's bench for the second year. Daddy said we had to go back, because we didn't get religion the first time, or as daddy would say, "You don't have anything". I accepted Jesus on July 29th, 1954, and my parents knew it. Daddy would get on his knees every night to pray. He and Madear would get on their knees on Sunday mornings and pray aloud. I know he learned that from his parents, because his mother, Mama Lottie would get up on Sunday mornings and pray aloud.

I knew my dad, a man called Mama, was not a perfect man, and was not without sin (Romans 3:23-24). A man called Mama fathered a child (a son) by another woman, after having 11 children by our mother. He never mentioned a word to me, nor did my mother, being the gracious mother (woman) that she was. I am not sure when Madear found out.

Being Strict

Even though Daddy appeared to be very strict, he really wasn't. He could be classified as easy going, even though he would sound rough at times. As young children growing up at home, he never talked to us about the birds and bees. I think it was because of his old-fashioned way of being raised. It wasn't something his parents talked about, so he didn't either. He still allowed us to go out with friends, and even on dates.

He loved and liked Tim (my date) very much. Maybe because he knew his parents very well. Before he could take me out, Tim had to come to the house and ask Daddy if he could have my company. Tim and I got married on August 1st, 1962. Having a girl's company in those days was another way of going steady, which meant only seeing that one person. It also meant to the parents that if the girl got pregnant the boy that asked for the company was automatically assumed to be the daddy, and there was no way of denying or getting around it. When returning from a date Daddy would not allow us to sit in the car out in the yard. Once you arrived home you had to go inside as soon as your date brought you home.

Giving Sound Advice

Daddy, a man called Mama, was always concerned about the welfare of his children. Even in the 1960s, and onward, he continued to give advice. Even though I was the second one to leave home, he found himself giving advice just as often as before. Madear asked our cousin Maurine Wilburn if I could stay with them for the summer. She said yes, and Daddy agreed, but not before laying out his rules. Daddy said, "Girl you go down there and do the right thing. Be respectable and do what you're told to do. Don't be fast, and girl don't you be staying out late at night. Don't hang around the wrong people, don't let anybody make a fool out of you, and don't take any wooden nickels".

A Surprise Party

We never had birthday parties as kids at home. Our mother decided to have a surprise birthday party for Daddy in 1983 for his 70th birthday. We had a wonderful time planning and trying to keep it a secret. We thought it wouldn't be hard to do because he had gotten up early and gone to the barbershop, so we had all day to plan it. She invited friends and family. Daddy had a cousin named Man (Richard) Newsome who decided to tell him and spoiled the surprise. When Daddy came home, he had to act as if he was really surprised. Later he told Madear what had happened.

The following is daddy's description of his life as a drinker. His words were not edited. He titled it:

Subject of My Life When I Was Drinking,
J.D. Newsome

Part 1

Once upon a time I was a drinker. I would drink every day and a lot of days I would get drunk and some days I would get high. Sometimes I would go to sleep sit up in my car. I remember one evening just about time to turn on my car lights, I turn off the main highway on another road, and my car motor fell dead. I didn't know where I was going. I sit up in my car and went to sleep. I had $16 in my pocket, I taken $3 out and put in my ash tray in my car door. That was before I left town. I went to sleep and when I woke up somebody had done hit me on my hand and my hand was all swollen up. It was 4 o'clock a. m. in the morning. Then I went to a cousin's house and got him to help me start my car. I got him to help me start because when my car motor fell dead, I didn't cut my lights off, and that run my car battery down and I couldn't start it, and my $13 was gone and my bill folder was out of my pocket in the seat with me, and my hat was in the back. Well after I got started, I went home my wife ask me where I had been, I couldn't tell her. I talked to myself about that, and said I was going to stop drinking. I would be sick for 2 or 3 days when I would drink a lot, but I didn't stop then. *So, I said if you drank stop, and if you don't, don't start because it's hell.*

Part 2

But I didn't stop then, every week I would drink. I came home one evening drunk, and my wife and kids wanted to go to the school program, and I didn't want to go, and didn't go. They went and I decided I would lay down, and I did and went to sleep on the porch and when they got back and woke me up, I got up and went in the house and went to bed. *Again, I say if you drank stop, and if you don't, don't start because it's hell*.

Once my cousin and myself bought 4 fifths of wine. 2 bottles we bought we drank those 2 bottles up in town and when we were on our way home, we open the other 2 and drank some out of one of them and we had only one left, he said it was his and I said it was mine, so there we started raising sand (trouble or fuss) about it. He snatched it run around the house and hide it in a tree hollow. Then the next day I went to town looking for me some more to drank, and I did get it. I would put a dime or 25 cents with the other boys and get it. Most of the time I would have my own money to get it with, and when I did, I would slip away and buy it and drank it by myself. When they see me again, I would be high, and we would start raising hell again. *So, if you drank, stop, and if you don't drank, don't start because it's hell.*

My prayers, one thing I didn't forget it was my prayers it didn't make no difference about how much I would drink, when I would get ready to go to bed, I would get on my knees to say my prayers. Many times, I would go to sleep on my knees saying my prayers, my wife would wake me up, and when she couldn't wake me up, I would be on my knees until the next morning. Sometimes she could wake me up, and sometimes she couldn't. When I would wake up, I would ask her why she didn't wake me up, and she would say "I tried to wake you up, but I couldn't". *So, I say If you drank stop, and if you don't drink, don't start, because it's hell.*

About the difference in stores, sometimes my wife would be with me when I would be in town, I would go to one store to buy some beer she would shake her head to the beer man not to sell me none and he wouldn't, and I would go to another to buy some beer to drank and she would do the same thing to the beer man not to let me have none.

About eating when I drank too much...............

This is where our daddy stopped writing about his life when he was drinking, and he never completed his story.

Life After The Farm Ended

Mama had a special place in the house where he spent most of his time a big recliner chair in the living room by the window where he would sit, not so much watching television, but dipping his snuff or chewing tobacco, and periodically calling out to Madear (whose name was Ina) "Uhhhhh IInaaa!" She would answer, and he would say, "Awe shit woman I can't hear you!!!!!" That's because she was soft spoken.

I know my dad, a man called Mama, loved all of his children -even though he never expressed those words. All of us knew our oldest brother Robert was his favorite child, but there was never any jealousy or hatred shown by any of us. I was very close to him, and he had a special place in his heart for me, his second oldest, but that was never talked about or expressed; it was just something I always knew. When I would have to take him to the hospital, while visiting with him he would tell the nurses, "That's my daughter! She's a nurse!" You could tell he was proud of all of his children and our accomplishments.

Mama had a unique personality. His vocabulary was like none other with his profanity, being comical, and serious too. He had many slang words and curse words that you never heard from anybody or anywhere else. He would still read his bible though, and his favorite scripture was Psalm 27 in its entirety. He was reared up in Washington County in a little town called Chappell Hill, Texas, where he learned to speak Polish very well, surrounded by Polish people. At times, a man called Mama could be thought of as a man with few words. Then there were other times, when he was quite verbal.

Mama did not like to travel very much. Once, he agreed to fly to Kansas City, MO but only if he could ride the train back home, and he did. He was a barber (the only barber), in downtown Chappell Hill -in the same shop where his uncle had been a barber many years ago. Daddy would travel downtown on Saturdays, and almost every weekday -Sunday mornings only by request. He would regularly cut hair, but also shaved beards and mustaches on request. He only had a seventh-grade education.

There were some who thought that the Newsome's were rich, while others wondered how Daddy was able to take care of all of his children. He was an entrepreneur too, and he kept very meticulous records -not just from his hair cutting, but also from the many times he sold hogs, as well as from the food he purchased for them. I think my record keeping today came from my dad. The records are still in our possession today, showing his fees as small as 50 cents for cutting hair, and their gradual increase over the years. He would cut hair without immediate pay, extending credit to many. I would see some of my friends in town on Saturdays, and we would go to my dad's shop, and he would trim their edges without charging them. Even close family members would not get charged at all or would pay a reduced fee.

Our dad, a man called Mama, never earned a lot of money, but one thing I can attest to is that he was a good provider for his family. We always had food to eat. I don't remember ever being hungry or going without food. However, there were times during the harvest season (taking cotton to the cotton gin), he would surprise us by buying or new clothing or something special to eat.

Our dad suffered from Chronic Obstructive Pulmonary Disease (COPD), a lung disease from years of smoking, and emphysema, also a lung disease that causes shortness of breath (SOB). When he stopped smoking his lungs were already damaged, and that could not be reversed, causing him to be put on oxygen at home. After wearing oxygen daily, Mama discontinued going to his shop to cut hair, but he would accept customers at home and continued to work. When Mama was no longer able to cut hair, he was pretty sedentary. He had a big chair that sat right by the living room window where he spent most of his days watching very little television while chewing tobacco and dipping snuff.

He smoked and drank for many years before his death. He stopped smoking without any Nicotine Replacement Therapy (seeking professional help), and stopped drinking without the help of AA as well.

One Saturday, after I had visited my parents all day, I recall Daddy appeared to have had a normal day without any respiratory distress. Later that evening, after I had gone home, he experienced some shortness of breath, and even though he was wearing his oxygen he suffered acute respiratory failure, and as a result he went into respiratory arrest at home. Our sister Joyce who lived next door resuscitated him by doing rescue breathing until EMS arrived. They took him to the hospital in Brenham, Texas where he died 3 days later.

Did You Know Daddy.........

- Played softball in school
- Could draw
- Could sing
- Only completed the 7th grade (even though he was an entrepreneur and a meticulous record keeper)
- Worked at the 7-UP Plant in Houston
- Used to work for the railroad (periodically they would have issues on the track, and would hire extra people, they would be called extra-gang), and that's why his social security # started with a 7 (721) and not a 4), because prior to 1963, railroad employees were assigned a Social Security number starting with 3 digits ranging from 700-728

SPINN. EHLERT. SPINN. WEISLER & WEISLER
ATTORNEYS - AT - LAW
115 East Main St.
P.O. Box 1118
Brenham, Texas 77833

LAST WILL AND TESTAMENT
OF
J.D. NEWSOME

THE STATE OF TEXAS I

COUNTY OF WASHINGTON I

KNOW ALL MEN BY THESE PRESENTS:

That I, J. D. Newsome, of Washington County, Texas, being of sound mind and memory, and being desirous to provide for the disposition of my property and estate at my death, do hereby make, publish and declare this to be my last will and testament, and hereby expressly any and all other wills and codicils by me at any time heretofore made.

I.

I desire and direct that my body be buried in a decent and Christian-like manner, suitable to my circumstances and condition in life, the expenses of same to be paid out of my estate by my hereinafter named Executrix as soon as my death is practical.

II.

I desire and direct that all my debts, if any there be, be paid out of my estate by my hereinafter named Executrix as soon as practical, but nothing herein shall require my Executrix to pay any debt or claim barred by any applicable statute of limitation or in advance of maturity.

III.

I wish to state that I have acquired my separate property upon which I reside and declare to be my homestead located in the James Stevens League, Washington County, Texas.

I do hereby give , bequeath and devise all my said real property consisting of seven acres, more or less, unto my beloved wife, Ina Newsome, to have and enjoy for and during the term of her natural life, together with all rights, uses and benefits, duties and obligations incidents to such estate as such term and interest is known at law, and at the death of my wife, Ina Newsome, in fee simple to my following children, Robert Lee Newsome, Johnnie Mae Newsome Lewis, Sterling Newsome, Joe Gene Newsome, Edward James Newsome, Travis Newsome, Jerry Newsome, John Daniel Newsome, Delores F. Newsome, and Oscar W. Newsome, share and share alike, intending hereby to vest upon the date of my death, my interest in such real estate hereinabove described in said named children, in fee simple, subject however to the life estate herein devised in favor of my beloved wife Ina Newsome.

I wish to state that I have one child not named above, being my daughter Joyce Newsome Little, to whom I have previously given 0.25 acres out of said homestead tract, and for that reason have not included her in above device to my remaining
children.

IV.

I do hereby give, bequeath and devise unto my children namely, Robert Lee Newsome, Johnnie Mae Newsome Lewis, Sterling Newsome, Joe Newsome, Edward James Newsome, Joyce Newsome Little, Travis Newsome, Jerry Newsome, John Daniel Newsome, Delores F. Newsome, and Oscar W. Newsome, the rest, residue and remainder of my property and estate, whether real or personal, separate or community, or of whatsoever kind or character, or wheresoever located, in fee simple share and share alike, to sell, manage, of dispose of by deed will or otherwise, as they may see fit or deem proper.

V.

I do hereby constitute and appoint Ina Newsome, as Independent Executrix of this my last will and testament, and direct that no bond or other security shall be required of her as such and that no action be had in the Probate Court or any other court in connection with my estate other than to probate and record this will and return an inventory, appraisement and list of claims of my estate as required by law. In event Ina Newsome for any reason, be unable or unwilling to qualify as such Executrix, then in that event, I do hereby constitute and appoint Johnnie Mae Newsome Lewis as the Independent Executrix of this my last will and testament, and direct that no bond or other security shall be required of her as such and that no action be had in the probate or other court in connection with my estate other than to probate this will and return an inventory, appraisement and list of claims as required by law.

IN WITNESS WHEREFORE, I have hereunto set my name in the presence of the two subscribing witnesses, who attest the same as witnesses at my request and in my presence, and in the presence of each other, on this 5th day of June, 1981

J. D. Newsome
J. D. Newsome, Testator

The above and foregoing instrument was now here subscribed by J. D. Newsome, then Testator, in our presence, and we, at his request and in his presence, and in the presence of each other, sign our names hereto as attesting and subscribing witnesses on this the 5th day of June, 1981.

Mary Bentley
Mary Bentley

Janice Fairlie
Janice Fairlie

SELF PROVING AFFIDAVIT

THE STATE OF TEXAS I
COUNTY OF WASHINGTON I

Before me, the undersigned authority, on this day personal appeared J. D. Newsome, Mary Bentley and Janice Fairlie, known to me to be the Testator and the two witnesses, respectively, whose names are subscribed to the foregoing or annexed instrument, in their respective capacities, and all of said persons being by me duly sworn, the said J. D. Newsome, Testator, declared to me and the said witnesses, in my presence, that said instrument is the last will and testament, and that he had willingly made and executed it as his free act and deed for the purposes therein expressed; and the said witnesses, each on his/her oath, stated to me in the presence and hearing of the said Testator, that the said Testator, had declared to them that the instrument is the last will and testament, and that he executed the same as such and wanted each of them to sign it as a witness;

and upon their oaths, each witness further stated that they did sign the same as witnesses in that he was, at that time, eighteen years of age or over, and was of sound mind; that each of said witnesses was then at least fourteen years of age.

J. D. Newsome

J. D. Newsome,

TESTATOR

Mary Bentley

Mary Bentley,

Witness

Janice Fairlie

Janice Fairlie,

Witness

Subscribed and acknowledged before me by the said J.D. Newsome, Testator, and subscribed and sworn to before me by the said Mary Bentley and Janice Fairlie, Witnesses, on this the 5th day of June, 1981.

Paul A. Ehleat

Notary Public in and for
the State of Texas

(Seal was Placed Here)

CHAPTER 3
Sterling Newsome

Who has ever heard of a man being called 'Mama'? Mama is a name for a mother...not a name for a man. I know I have never heard of such a thing! Why would such a name be given to a man? Well, this man was my daddy, and I never called him anything but "Daddy." Still, almost everyone in our small town of Chappell Hill, Texas called him Mama. Daddy never had a problem with that name. He always answered to that name when people called him Mama. Hardly anyone called him by his given name, John (John Douglas). There were probably many people who never knew what his real name was.

The story I was told was that when my daddy was a little boy, his father tagged that name. He was given that name because he had an identical twin brother who was given the name, "Papa," and this was the way the parents would tell the boys apart. Their father (Philip) did not have a car, but he had horses he rode to every place he needed to go. He even used the horses to plow the cotton field. During harvest time, Philip used a horse to take the cotton to the gin.

My daddy and his brother always looked forward to this time because they knew their father would bring candy and other goodies back home for them. They wanted to go with him to the gin, but they were too small to go. To make the boys happy, he would place the boys on his knee and bounce them up and down as if they were riding a horse. As they bounced up and down, Philip would sing a song: "Get up horse, Mama and Papa going to town and get some candy. Get up horse, Mama and Papa going to town and get some candy!"

I grew up in the shadow of my daddy. I saw him as a "real man." He was a kind man. He was a no-nonsense man who did not "take any stuff" off anyone. He disciplined his children when it was appropriate. He taught us religious values. He knew the value of having a personal relationship with God and he wanted to make sure that his children knew what it meant to have such a relationship. He read and studied his Bible and helped to lay a good foundation for his family. For my daddy, developing a solid connection with God was serious business. I know when I confessed a personal relationship with Jesus, Daddy looked me in my eyes and pointed his fingers at me and said, "Boy, you make sure you got religion!" For Daddy, this meant I needed to be sure that there was no doubt that I had accepted Jesus as Lord and Savior of my life.

My daddy was a good man, but he was not a perfect man. He worked hard for his family. He worked the fields. He was a barber who made sure that all his eight boys' hair was cut. He walked more than a mile to town to his shop to cut the hair of his customers. He purchased a car later so the family could have transportation to school, church, work, and to other places. I was very concerned with my daddy because sometimes he would drink and drive. I recall one time when he had too many beers, drove home, and fell asleep in the yard with his face on the horn.

I never heard Daddy talk about that incident. He was probably disappointed in himself. I know he was disappointed with me a few years later when he found out about some of the habits I had developed. But he never gave up on me. He still prayed for me and gave me sound counsel.

He was always a business-minded person. He always worked for himself. He kept detailed ledgers and notes about his business activities. He kept copious notes of financial matters. I am certain that his ways of doing business were an inspiration to me and other members of my family as we operated our own businesses and as we got degrees in finance, engineering, law, business administration, and operated real estate and appraisal firms. I can recall early on, as a teenager, running a corner store in Chappell Hill, where we sold refreshments and played music on a victrola record player. Later, I operated a body shop for many years. It was not that Daddy sat down and talked about doing any of these things, but there was something instilled in our brains about the necessity of having our own businesses and being in control of our own future. The little corner store did not turn out to be a franchise, but Daddy had planted a seed in all our heads about the importance of entrepreneurship. I am forever grateful to my father for his leadership.

Daddy was witty and always gave wise counsel. He was always wary of people who would not look him in the eye when having a conversation. He'd say to me: "Son, don't take no wooden nickels off anyone." If there was a certain person who was bragging about himself or his possessions, I would ask Daddy if that person was about anything. Dad would say, "He is trying to be big, but little is eating his ass up!" I remember a time when Daddy and I were having a conversation and I asked him about how I should respond to a person who is known for not telling the truth. His response was, "Hunch yourself and wink your eye at the world." Then I asked him what the phrase meant, and he said it meant absolutely nothing.

My daddy was human. The man called Mama was my daddy. He was also the daddy of my half-brother whom he loved just the same as he loved all his other eleven children. Daddy and I never had any conversation about his ninth son, my half-brother, but knowing my daddy, he would be thrilled to know that I love my half-brother just as I love the rest of my siblings.

Daddy never denied the existence of his son, nor did he confirm it, but that does not matter now. What's done is done and the legacy of my daddy will continue to survive through all of us.

CHAPTER 4
Joe Gene Newsome

GET UP HORSES GOING TO TOWN, BUY SOME CANDY, GIVE NOBODY NONE; I heard this name came from a trip my grandma used to take to town, when she would take the boys to town with her. When she got to town with the twins on her lap and no one could tell them apart, grandma (Mama Lottie) said this is Mama and this is Papa. So, my dad's name was John Douglas Newsome (Mama), and his twin brother's name was James Columbus Newsome (Papa). Daddy (Mama) as far as I can remember always lived in Chappell Hill Texas. For years we always got around in a wagon, and no it was not a covered wagon. I can always remember going to Sauney Stand, Texas, which was approximately five miles away. We had cousins in that area, and that is where our grandparents lived (Daniel Turknett) on my mother's side, so Dad would always drive us there. I also remember going to chop cotton and pick cotton down by the Brazos River, which was about six miles east on highway 290, headed toward Houston, Texas. Again, the wagon was our only source of transportation with the exception of riding a horse. (No, we did not have a saddle, just a cotton sack on the horse's back.)

We lived in a small shack, approximately two miles from downtown Chappell Hill, Texas, with no running water or electric lights. I don't remember the date, but Dad (Mama) at some point built us another house there on the land which he owned, that was given to him by his mom (Mama Lottie).

Dad farmed, raising hogs, chickens, ducks, and guinea pigs. We also had cows, a couple of horses, and a mule. There were also always plenty of other creatures around such as snakes, bull frogs, pee frogs, possums, armadillos, chichi birds, and buzzards. Dad used to butcher the hogs. We had a smokehouse where we would put all the meat from the hogs to cure.

Often the horses would get out of the pasture and venture down the gravel road and Dad would make us go and get them. One time we were chasing the horse and I picked up a rock and threw it at the horse and I was kicked in the face by that same horse! Another time, a cow got her legs tangled in the barbed-wire fence, and I was asked to help the cow get untangled. Once the leg was free, I got kicked in the chest.

I think Daddy had Edward in charge of the chickens one day, and he was told to go and get this rooster out of the cornfield. He returned from the cornfield and said he could not get the rooster because it had climbed up the cornstalk and would not come down. Daddy used one of his favorite words and told him, "Boy, get your shittin'-ass out there and get that rooster!"

There was a small pond in the area, and Daddy always told us, "Don't take your ass down to that pond!" fearing that we would fall in and drown. Sure, enough, when I was a small boy, they say I tried walking across the pond to retrieve a duck that had gone into the water, and I only survived thanks to our 1st cousin John Newsome who came in and got me from the pond.

Daddy was a barber, a farmer, and I think he tinkered with trying to make some alcohol once (I saw that gadget too). One thing for sure, we always had a fresh haircut when we went to church and school. Daddy had a small barber shop in downtown Chappell, TX which I visited sometimes, but we always got our hair cut at home. On Saturdays, we would go to town to visit him, and he would give us a nickel to buy Jack cookies; mm... they were so good! On the way to town to visit Daddy we would always pass the service station called Buckeye and Lucy's grocery store, and they would always ask "Y'all Mama's boys?" We had strict instructions not to be talking back to those 'white folk'.

Daddy used to go to town almost every day. I can hear him saying, "Ina(mom) I`m going up town." He always wore a white shirt, and mostly gray or black slacks with black suspenders.

He always told us to keep our clothes clean and to not leave home in dirty underclothes, because you might get sick and have to go to the hospital, and you should have on clean draws.

Dad taught us to not be talking back to people, especially to those white folk. Even after we had left Chappell Hill and moved to Kansas City, Missouri and went back and forth to Chappell Hill to visit, we'd go up town to the store and he would say "Don't y'all be up there showing out and getting smart with those white folks because we have to live with them."

Daddy smoked, and he used to roll his cigarettes. He kept a can of Prince Albert tobacco. Daddy also would drink beer, and sometimes he would have a bottle or two too many and would come home a little tipsy. Oh, yeah, he would curse as well, and he had plenty of choice words like damn, hell, and shittin'-ass. We were not allowed to curse or say words that sounded like curse words. Daddy would dare us to curse or say a bad word. If we got angry with him about something he would say "Curse me and die! I brought you into this world and I will take you out!"

Some of Daddy's favorite sayings were, "You want to be big, but little is biting you all in the ass!"; "Hunch yourself and wink your eye at the world."; "Piss poor"; and "Lord, help Jesus!". Dad would always say, "Don't y'all go around bothering people but don't take no wooden nickels."

Dad was Baptist and we were Methodist. Our churches were about a 1/2 a mile apart, and we pretty much went every Sunday, however he didn't go as often.

Just an Educated Fool

In our younger days, we were told about accepting Jesus. In order to do that you'd have to go to the mourners bench during the time revival was being held. You were required to separate yourself from family and friends and go off and pray. You'd either lock yourself in a quiet place or walk to the woods and pray. Daddy would always drive us to church for revival. I don't remember Daddy staying for the revival service, as the matter of fact I don't ever remember Daddy ever visiting our church (St. John AME Methodist Church).

Dad taught us how to farm, plant cotton, corn, and potatoes, and how to plow the field, slop the hogs, and milk the cows. He showed us how to draw water from the well and sift the weavers and bugs and leaves out of the water that had fallen in the well. Daddy planted cotton and corn, and at cotton picking time we would pick cotton. Once we got a wagon load, he would take it to the Gin house to sell. He would let us ride on the wagon with him and buy us a piece of candy or some cookies.

After we had harvested our cotton, which wasn't very much, Daddy would take us to pick cotton for others in the immediate area. Very little money was made. We got paid by the number of pounds picked, but we had to work to help him support the rest of the family. Once the cotton was picked in the area, we would go on a cotton pick which was 400 to 500 miles away. We would travel all night in the back of a covered truck. I was around 12-15 years old. Once we arrived at our destination the owner of the cottonfield had a small house where we would stay for 3 to 5 weeks picking cotton and making money to bring home to Daddy to buy our school clothes. Of course, this caused us to start school late every year. We were transported to these locations (Lubbock, TX and Muleshoe, TX) by Mr. Timothy and C L Lewis who turned out to be my sister Johnnie Newsome-Lewis' in-laws. Daddy had us chopping cotton, and bailing hay. Many days we would be working and could see and hear other kids at school during recess time. When we got off early, we had to pass the school, so we would scoot down in our seats in the car so the kids could not see us when we passed by. The teacher would always ask where we had been.

How did Daddy affect yesterday and today? I can remember Daddy calling us early in the morning, and saying, "Y`all get up!", so we could go to the fields, either to chop or to pick cotton. Always before we went to work, he'd say, "Don't forget to slop (feed) the hogs before we leave to work!" We would mix the grain with water and walk down to the hog pen and fill the hog craw with food.

Daddy had us doing what we could to help, picking cotton, chopping cotton, pulling corn, picking pecans, bailing hay, and so on. When we would pick berries, we would go down the dirt road and find a berry patch and pick dewberries. Sometimes, we would walk along the railroad track and pick berries, all the while chasing snakes around the vines. We would take the berries to the highway and stand on the side of the highway and sell berries. We sold them for $3.00 per gallon or a small container for less. The only highway that came through town was Highway 290, which ran from Houston, Texas, 60 miles east of our hometown, to Brenham, Texas, 10 miles west of us. There was always plenty of traffic to whom we could sell the berries.

It would be so hot standing on the side of the highway, and when the cars and trucks passed, they would always give a nice gust of hot air. The most pleasant part was when a car would stop and ask how much we wanted per gallon, and when they'd let their window down, all of that cool air would give you a few seconds of fresh air.

Daddy would always say "Don't go across the road in Mr. Whitney's pasture to fish or pick pecans off of his trees" but one night after dark Sterling and I went anyway. We were picking pecans and we heard a voice say, "WHAT are you boys doing picking my pecans!!" It was Mr. Whitney riding a horse, and off we went running! As we were running, we got caught in the barbed wire fence. I don't remember the result with Mr. Whitney, but it wasn't good with Daddy! "I told y`all not to take y`all shittin'-asses over there in that man's pasture!" WHEW!

AUTOBIOGRAPHY (Joe Gene Newsome)

I was born in Chappell Hill, Texas, a small town approximately 60 miles west of Houston, Texas. There I lived in a small farm-type house with my mom and dad and siblings. I worked on the family farm and in the surrounding areas. I graduated from C. H. Hogan High School in June of 1961 with a 10th grade education. Upon graduation I moved to Kansas City, Missouri to live with my brothers Robert and Sterling.

Sterling and I lived with Robert and Wilma, his wife, for a short time until we rented a kitchenette from a Mr. and Mrs. Tinsley, at 4004 Prospect Avenue. There I continued my education, going to Westport High School at night to finish the 11th and 12th grade. After that, I went to Penn Valley Community College and took drafting but did not complete a degree.

I worked several small jobs- as a busboy, dishwasher, and a small fry cook, before going to work at Montgomery Wards in the stock room. Later I would work at Chicago Title Insurance where I learned all about legal description, lots and blocks, and how to do a chain of title to establish legal ownership of real estate. Finally, in 1977, I got my Real Estate License, and I sold Real Estate from 1977 to 1984. I began to help my brother Robert as a Real Estate Appraiser. I got all of my training and classes completed and currently continue to be an appraiser. Though I still do appraisal, I mostly buy and flip houses with my two daughters.

My hobbies consist of bicycle riding, walking, and playing cards, spades, and bid whiz. I started bowling in league competition in 1969, where I have averaged 200 during most of my bowling career. I've had 63 perfect games and have been inducted into the Kansas City, Missouri bowling Hall of Fame, the State of Missouri Hall of Fame, The National Bowling Association Hall of Fame, and the Kansas City Black Archives. I still travel to different cities nationwide to participate in bowling tournaments.

I also enjoy working with my church every third Wednesday passing out food that has been provided by harvesters to the community.

I am currently the President of the Greater Kansas City, Missouri Bowling Senate.

I attend United Community Church along with my daughter, her husband, and my three granddaughters.

I attend the softball games and basketball games of my granddaughters as often as possible.

CHAPTER 5
Edward J. Newsome

This chapter is dedicated to my father, mother, late brother Robert, and the rest of my wonderful siblings.

My disclaimer: To the best of my knowledge and ability, every word in this writing is accurate. You have always heard that "truth is stranger than fiction"; therefore, I am sticking to the truth because somebody cannot make up the history of my daddy – I can only tell it from my point of view.

"Behold, children are a heritage from the Lord; the fruit of the womb is a reward. Like arrows in the hand of a warrior, so are the children of one's youth. Happy is the man who has his quiver full of them; they shall not be ashamed but shall speak with the enemies in the gate." Psalms 127:3-5

My mama or my daddy?
A man called Mama is my daddy, not my mama. He never tried to be my mama; our mother did very well. Why would a man be called Mama, anyway? Mama would be considered a nickname.

My daddy's given name was John Douglas Newsome. He had three brothers whose names were James Columbus Newsome ("Papa" or "Uncle J.C.;"), Audie Dell Newsome ("Uncle Dell"), and Willie Bee ("Bull Jones") Newsome. James Columbus ("Papa") and Daddy were identical twins...I do mean the same! Except for one little thing: Mama was left-handed, and Papa was right-handed. Other than that, they were so much alike that even many times, I could not tell them apart. Their appearances confused me as a little child and many others as adults, especially when Daddy and uncle were together.

Mama Lottie, the mother of these four children, had her nickname: "Sa- Lottie." I never heard anyone call her that except the four sons. My mother only called Daddy "J.D." and nothing else. Daddy called Madear "Ina," which was her first name. He said he called her Ina because if another name like "Honey" or "Baby" was used and he had one day come home and forgotten to call her those sweet names, she might've thought he was angry at her or that he had been doing something wrong. To him, that made a lot of sense. It may not make sense to anyone else. I just took him at his word.

My mother had a middle name, but I never knew how to spell it. I think it was "Authonia," but I am unsure because she would not tell me when I asked her how to spell it. Having somewhat unusual names in my family is par for the course because my mother's maiden name was "Turknett;" people called her father "Papa Turknett." My parents didn't like nicknames so none of their 11 children had nicknames. My daddy was the only person in the world who called me by my middle name, "James."

"You don't raise heroes; you raise sons. And if you treat them like sons, they'll become heroes, even if it's just in your own eyes." -Walter M. Schirra, Sr.

Mama, Mama Lottie

As legend would have it, the story goes like this: When Mama Lottie, our grandmother, was raising the twins, sometimes she would get them mixed up. Whenever she called out for one or the other, she would say, "come here to me, boy!" But she wanted the other boy to come to her. Then, one day, she did something different to help her remember which boy was which. She tied a white string on one boy's finger and a black one on the others. The boy with the white string sat on her left knee, and she called him "Mama." The boy with the black string sat on her right knee and she called him "Papa." Then she made up a song like this: *"I'm going downtown to buy some candy, ain't gonna give nobody none but Mama and Papa. Giddy up horsey, giddy up, take me downtown to buy some candy for Mama and Papa."*The strings stayed on the boys' fingers for a long time, long enough for her to distinguish one from the other. And, as she was singing the song, she would bounce the boys up and down on her knees as if they were riding a horse.

The names stuck with my daddy and his brother. Every person in the town who knew my dad knew him as Mama Newsome. When somebody spoke that name, there was never a question of about whom they were speaking. For my siblings and me, it was only Daddy.

"The wisest of women builds her house, but folly with her own hands tears it down." – Proverbs 14:1

Mama, Oh, Mama!
Suffice it to say Mama Lottie was a legend long before her time. She has a story that's worth telling. She used to say, "I ain't gonna take no shit off that bitch or the horse she rode in on!" Well, as the story goes, *"that bitch"*-a lady who will go unnamed and will only be known as "Ms. J.," made it a practice of entertaining a man named Phillip Newsome, called "Daddy Bud," who just happened to be united in holy matrimony to Mama Lottie. He was also my grandfather.

Let me paint the picture very clearly. According to county records and legal documents, my grandfather and grandmother purchased a piece of land, 30.4 acres, in the County of Washington and the City of Chappell Hill in the summer of 1929, just as the Great Depression was coming on. Times were tough, not just for my grandparents, but for everybody, black and white, rich and poor. Research shows that the worst of the Great Depression was between 1932 and

1933, just after my grandparents purchased their land. Due to the lack of work and steady income, they fell far behind on land payments. My grandmother decided she needed to work to save the land from foreclosure. She got word of a white lady needing a maid; however, the job was in Fort Worth, Texas, about 200 miles northeast of Chappell Hill. Having no other options, around 1932, my grandmother boarded a train to Fort Worth, took the job, and started working as a maid for a family on Primrose Street. She lived in the house with the family and worked day and night, night and day, seven days a week. She pocketed every penny she made to save the land they had bought for the family. My grandfather worked odd jobs but needed to make more money to keep up with the payments on the ground—more money than my grandmother was making was required to catch up and get ahead. Several years passed, and they fell further behind with the land payment. Having land was important, especially for Black people, and especially during a time when many Blacks were sharecropping and living on the land of the white landowner. Mama Lottie wanted more than that for her family. Legal papers show that due to a lack of payments from 1930 to 1934, and after many demands, the landowner, Mr. Joe K., filed a foreclosure notice against my grandparents. My grandmother had made enough money to hold off the foreclosure and saved the land. Around 300,000 companies went out of business.

Hundreds of thousands of families could not pay their mortgages. Millions of families migrated from their homes to the Midwest and other regions. In light of all of this, this showed the resolve my grandmother had. In the meantime, my grandfather was still around town doing his thing. Legend has it that he rode a horse and carried a pistol, a Bible, a blanket, and a set of dice. There was never a time nor a reason for him not to make a little money here or there. He was a hustler! He had another little habit. Word was seeping out all over town that he was having a little fling. This episode occurred while my grandmother worked hard in Fort Worth to make enough money to save the family farm. When the word got back to my grandmother, she hopped on a train and returned home to end all the shenanigans. She got off the train, walked downtown, spotted Ms. J. on the street next to Mr. P. Lesser's store, walked up to her, and without saying a word, snatched her from behind, nearly tearing off her dress, then hauled off and slapped the living daylight out of Ms. J., knocking her glasses to the ground. Ms. J. never said a single word, nor did my grandmother have a word to say, not while standing there.

However, she had other things on her mind. My grandmother then walked down the street to the Justice of the Peace office and said to the officer, *"I just slapped the shit out of that bitch for messing with my husband, and there ain't nothing you gonna do to me!"* The officer looked at her and said, *"Okay, Ms. Lottie!"* Then, she walked to the pool hall where my grandfather, her husband, usually hung out, walked up to him, and said, *"I just slapped your bitch from here to kingdom come...you might want to go out and pick that piece of shit up off the ground!"* My grandmother never had to worry about that situation again because she got rid of her husband and never looked back. My daddy was about 21 years old at that time. He never had much to say about this incident, but he knew his mother did not take any stuff from anyone.

The land she bought had two houses on it. When she returned from working in Fort Worth, the larger house was a place for her to live. Her oldest son and his family lived in the house for a while when she was gone. My father and mother later occupied the smaller house after they married in 1937, and it was there where they birthed 8 of their 11 children. My grandmother returned from Fort Worth around 1957 and lived in her house for a few years after her oldest son moved out. She died in a nursing home in Brookshire, Texas, on December 9th, 1972, at 87 years old.

"Then God blessed them, and said to them, 'Be fruitful and multiply; fill the earth and subdue it..." - Genesis 1:28 NKJV.

Mama, The House, & The Family that Mama Built

My family lived in the little unpainted house on the land my grandmother purchased, about two miles from downtown. The house was close to the dusty dirt road, and when cars and trucks passed, dust would circulate everywhere in the house. There were no utilities to the house. Having no utilities was typical for most older homes during that day. We used kerosene lamps for lighting; we used a long hemp rope and metal bucket to draw water from the deep well that was up near my grandmother's house; we used a four-eye wood stove with an oven for cooking; we had a potbelly wood heater sitting in the living room to provide warmth from the cold; we had an outhouse because there were no indoor toilets; we had a slop jar to pee in if nature called at night. These were all provisions made by my daddy for his family.

The old house by the road kept deteriorating as the family grew larger and larger. I never knew how my parents could have so many children in such a small house. All we knew was that a new baby would suddenly appear every couple of years. We didn't ask any questions; having babies just seemed like the natural thing to do. None of us were born in a hospital: we were all conceived and birthed with the assistance of a midwife. Did I ever see the midwife? My parents had a symmetric or palindromic order for having babies: one boy, one girl, three boys, one girl, three boys, one girl, and one boy (1-1-3-1-3-1-1). My parents were nothing short of geniuses! They could have run a secret service operation for the Pentagon.

In 1953, when I was seven years old, I helped my father build another house. The little bungalow was home but could not stand too much wind and rain. When there was rain, we put buckets on the floor to catch the water.

My father was afraid of storms, and when the clouds got dark, and the wind blew, he would grab the family and go up the hill to Mama Lottie's house until the storm was over. I remember in September of 1961, when Hurricane Carla -one of the strongest storms of the century, hit Texas; we went to my grandmother's house and did not go outside for three days. The little bungalow which we had abandoned withstood most of the damage, but all the inside was wet. Daddy and the family stayed in that little house until we built another bungalow in 1969. By then, five of the older siblings had left home for Houston and Kansas City.

In 1987, my siblings and I built a more ideal, sturdier brick home for our parents. This newer home is the home where they stayed until they died. I can still visualize Daddy sitting in his soft brown chair, looking out the windows; the spittle can he used to keep on the floor as he watched the cars pass by on the dusty unpaved road. Daddy was sitting in his chair the last time I saw him alive. I miss you, Mama Newsome. *"Daddy, do you love ME?"* He would still reply, *"Shit boy, don't keep asking me that; I already told you I love all of you!"*

"Who can find a virtuous wife?... She considers a field and buys it; from her profits, she plants a vineyard. She girds herself with strength and strengthens her arms.

She perceives that her merchandise is good." – Proverbs 31:10a; 16-18a

"A father doesn't tell you that he loves you. He shows you." – Demitri the Stoneheart.

Mama: What You Saw Was What You Got
I loved my daddy just how he was and for who and what he was. He was never affectionate, nor did he offer to say that he loved me. I don't know that I missed that because it was never something I had experienced from him in the first place. I don't remember how and when I thought those words were valuable. I knew he had eleven children, and he provided for each of us in the best way he could. He did not "model" his care, concern, and compassion affectionately, but he modeled his love by always being present in our home and doing his best to ensure we were all fed and had a roof over our heads.

My daddy not being an affectionate person was never something I held against him because that was not too unusual in that day and time for Black men. He was strong. He was a good man. He took care of his wife and children. I can never remember a time when Dad was not home at night. I can never remember when he was still in bed when I got up in the morning. The sun never caught Daddy in bed. He was up before the chickens and roosters. He was consistent. He was available. He always found a way to feed us when we lacked food. When we could not afford new shoes and clothes, he found a way to dress us; when we did not have money to go to the doctor, he found a way to heal us. He did not go past the third grade in school, but he knew how to read the Bible and educate us. My daddy found joy and happiness in teaching us.

"The greatest gift I ever had came from God;
I call him Dad!" - Anonymous Mama, The Shrewd

Mama: The Savvy Businessman
I could not have raised 11 children, provided for them, and kept them out of jail and hospital. Daddy was a sage and intelligent man. He never had to come to the schools and talk to the principal about us. We knew better than to act up or get out of place at school.

Daddy was a businessman. I once heard him say, *"Black folks don't have any business; they only have arrangements."* I never knew what he meant by that statement, but he certainly had business.

He was a bookkeeper. He had several little two-inch by four-inch ledgers where he kept copious and meticulous notes on every penny, he made cutting hair. He posted the date, the time, the name, and the amount of money each person paid him or owed him. He posted that in the little ledger if he loaned a person a quarter or dollar. He also posted that in the nominal ledger, if he borrowed a quarter or dollar from someone else. Daddy's philosophy about spending money*:* *"When your outgo is more than your income, you are in a helluva' fix!"*

"When my father didn't have my hand...he had my back." – Linda Poindexter.

Mama: The Clever Personality
Daddy was a religious man, but he did not always go to church. Yet, he had some very colorful language that he used very adroitly. Dad used curse words often and skillfully. He never cursed any of us children, but he would use curse words during his chastisement of us. I heard one person say that Daddy could curse someone out, and that person would walk away with a smile, thinking Daddy had complimented them. That's very clever!

"I cannot think of any need in childhood as strong as the need for a father's protection." – Sigmund Freud.

Mama: The GQ Guy

Daddy had a way of dressing about him. I never saw Daddy wear anything other than white shirts, whether going to the cotton field, plowing the field, going to church, cutting hair at the barber shop, or cutting hair on the sidewalk. I never saw Daddy wear any sneakers or tennis shoes. He always wore shined shoes or cowboy boots. His brand of choice was Stacy Adams keen-toed dress shoes. I never saw Daddy wear a cap of any kind. He always wore a short-brimmed hat. I never saw Daddy wear blue jeans, khakis, overalls, or coveralls. He only wore creased dress slacks. He worked as a clothes presser during his younger years. He was not into sports. I heard him say that if the World Series was played in his backyard, he would not watch it.

"My father used to say that it's never too late to do anything you want to do.
And he said, 'You never know what you can accomplish until you try.'" –Michael Jordan

Mama: The Hustler

Daddy was a hustler: a go-getter, an entrepreneur. He loved getting and "making money." I recall when he tried to "make money" by putting his "pressing skills" to use. He set up an ironing board or used a smooth, stable surface. Then he placed a lard paper on the ironing board, then put a denomination of money (dollar, five-, or ten-dollar bill, whatever bill he had) on top of the lard paper, then placed another piece of lard paper on top of the bill, then took the hot iron from the hot stovetop and slowly pressed over the lard paper several times until the imprint of the money melded (blended) onto the lard paper. Attempting to make money this way did not work out well. I did not assist in that venture.

However, Daddy did show us more legitimate ways to make money by gathering scrap iron and tin, loose rags and clothes, and when the scrap man came by looking for such products, we sold them and made the money for the family.

"Dad, your guiding hand on my shoulder will remain with me forever." – Author Unknown.

Mama: The True Edger

Daddy was rather ingenious when it came to barbering. He only sometimes cut hair inside his little one-room barber shop, especially if it was too hot. Dad would pull a chair or a bucket under a shade tree and ply his trade. Sometimes when Daddy was cutting hair and ran out of soap to make lather, he would pour beer into a cup and stir the beer with his little wiping mop until it made a lather. Dad then splattered either his finger or the little straw mop around the person's head. Then he would take his straight-edge razor, whip it up and down on his leather strop (a piece of leather for sharpening a straight razor) to make it sharp. Then he would take a long sip of the remaining beer from the can and then commence to shaving around the head of the person whose hair he was cutting. I don't know if he ever nicked anyone with the sharpened razor, but it would have been a miracle if he did not.

"I don't care how poor a man is; if he has family, he's rich." –M A S H, Colonel Potter.

Mama: The Gold Digger

He also tried mining or digging for money. I was a part of this venture. He had gotten wind from a particular "source" (a radio preacher) of some money being buried on a specific piece of property up in Burleson County, quite a distance from our home in Washington County. The "source" convinced Daddy to mail him a tiny bit of money, and he would send Daddy the location of the place and the money, plus Daddy would receive several "prayer cloths" to put in his pocket as a sign of good luck. Sure enough, Daddy got the location and directions for where we could find the money, plus the prayer cloths, which he shared with those of us on the dig with him.

Daddy assembled a team of two other people, along with me, and we went on the money-digging expedition. One of the problems was that we could only dig for the money at night and not dig past midnight. The supposed location where somebody had buried the money was on a white man's property, near the side of the road, under a big tree, in Burleson County. We set out on the expedition on a particular night. We followed the instructions from the source and found the place and the specific tree as had been described. We carried a dimly lit lantern, two shovels for digging, a burlap bag to hold the money, and our prayer cloths in our pockets. Another interesting tidbit, per our instructions, was that we were not allowed to talk while we were digging; if we spoke, the money would sink deeper into the ground. We developed a set of arcane hand signals to use for silent communication. As Daddy and the other two men dug and dug in the hard black soil, I held the burlap bag and the lantern, waiting to secure the spoils. Well, midnight came, and the only thing we uncovered was NOTHING! After a few days, Daddy reported to the source that we had found nothing. The one question from the source was, *"were all of the people involved in the expedition saved?"* Daddy responded that only one of the persons on the team was unsaved, at which time, the source replied: *"Yep, that was the reason you did not get the money!"* We never set out on such an expedition again. I kept my prayer cloth in my wallet for many years after I left home.

"Never raise your hand to your kids. It leaves your groin unprotected." –Red Buttons.

Mama: The Surprise Fighter

Daddy had other exciting events in his life, especially while drinking. I remember he got into a fight with one of his brothers-in-law, whose name will go unmentioned here. Daddy came home with a knot over his left eye and blood running down his forehead. There was never a conversation about what had transpired, but I noticed that Daddy kept his distance from my uncle, my mother's brother, for many years. There was another incident where Daddy had been drinking and had gotten into a fight with another person whom I will only refer to as "J.B." Again, Daddy came home with his face bleeding and swollen. He told us who did this to him. Even though this person has been dead for many years, I don't think I ever forgave him for beating up on my daddy. *(LORD, please forgive me for the anger that I have harbored against this person for so many years!).*

My mother was always displeased with my father's drinking. She may have reached her wit's end when Daddy came home so drunk one night that he tried to get inside the stove. He had no recollection of that unsuccessful entry. I learned from my daddy from that and other incidents that I would never be a drinker if that were how it made me behave. I have kept my word.

"My father didn't tell me how to live; he lived and let me watch him do it." –Clarence Budington Kelland.

Mama: Cold Turkey

A short time later, on July 10, 1955, Daddy stopped drinking "cold turkey" and never took another drink, as far as I know. But Daddy always smoked as far back as I can remember. His brand of choice was Prince Albert, an American hand-rolled cigarette and pipe tobacco brand introduced by the R.J. Reynolds Tobacco Company in 1907. I saw him roll and smoke many cigarettes! He did not allow any of us to smoke. But several of us tried to smoke anyway; however, we did not try Prince Albert. We tried the "natural brand"! We had a couple of horses on our little farm: Old Fannie and Trigger. Later, we got a horse named Silver. We would take a few dried horse droppings and roll them up in brown paper, much like Daddy rolled his Prince Albert tobacco inside the cigarette paper. Then we lit the horse-dried manured cigarette and started smoking. We never inhaled, but we did try to "make nicotine." This was a process whereby we drew from the cigarette, held the smoke in our mouths, put our mouths on the white bed sheet, and tried to see if we could make a brown spot. We never smoked this "product" again after sharing our little secret with one of our older first cousins, who then told Daddy, who commenced to spanking our bodies unmercifully. I will not reveal my cousin's name, but the next time I go to New York, somebody will have some 'splaining to do!

When Daddy stopped smoking, his habit became dipping snuff, a brand known as Levi Garrett, a loose-leaf chewing tobacco with a sweet flavor. Dad would take the grounded power tobacco and put it under his lip. After a few minutes, he would spit in a metal can or spit on the ground if outside. I chose not to follow my daddy with any of these habits.

"A good father is one of the most unsung, unpraised, unnoticed, and yet one of the most valuable assets in our society." – Billy Graham.

Mama: The Giver

Daddy's life impacted me in more ways than I can remember. I vaguely remember when Daddy took me on a trip to Galveston, Texas, on the train when I was six. We went to see his father, "Daddy Bud," who was hospitalized. Dad went to give him blood. I was too young to remember all the details of the trip. I don't know why he chose me to go with him. Going on the train with Daddy was the only time I remember doing anything alone with him or going anywhere with Daddy, except to the cotton field.

My mother prepared food for us to take on the train because, in those days, Blacks were not allowed to be served food on trains. She packed us six biscuits, fried chicken backs, a few wings, and a dozen teacakes, then double-wrapped the food in newspaper. I can still remember that the newspaper was greasy, but that did not matter to Daddy and me because we ate most of the food long before we reached our destination.

Neither Daddy nor I had a suitcase or luggage because the only clothes we took were the clothes we had on our backs. That was okay because we had not planned to stay in Galveston overnight. The plan was that Daddy would report to the hospital and give the blood while I waited outside in another room. These are details my daddy shared with me when I was older. It did not take long to give the blood to my grandfather, but he told me that when he came back to pick me up, I was curled up asleep in a chair.

I was not very observant at six years old, but I remember when we got off the train and walked to the hospital. We had to walk through an alley with tall apartments on both sides of the path. I recall there were people way up in the windows of the flats, and one person was hanging his head out of the window and throwing up. I felt a little queasy as Daddy and I walked by quickly, to avoid the person getting sick on our heads. For many years, I felt nauseous whenever I went to Galveston or thought about that place.
I do not remember when my grandfather died. I don't think he lived much longer after Daddy gave him the blood.

"I have found the best way to advise your children is to find out what they want and then advise them to do it." – Harry S. Truman.

Mama: The Adviser

When I was 17, I went with Madear on a train trip to St. Louis, Missouri. We were both delegates to a church convention. In St. Louis, we met my brother Robert, who was also in St. Louis, at a different church convention. When the sessions were over, Robert took Madear and me back to Kansas City in his new 1963 Dodge Dart. After spending the summer in Kansas City, I asked Daddy and Madear if I could stay in Kansas City and go to school. Daddy said I could, but that I needed to obey Robert and do what he told me.

Daddy always gave me plenty of advice. He always told me to be careful where I went and watch what I did. Dad warned me not to look up at the tall buildings while walking down the street because people would know I was from the country and take advantage of me. Further, he told me I should always remember the people who helped me along the way because it would be harder to be successful if I did not accept the help of others and if I did not provide support to others. He told me once he saw a turtle on the top of a fence post and knew there was no way for the turtle to get into that position without the help of someone else. I have always kept that vision in my head.

I went into the Army at the age of 21. Daddy advised me not to be doing any dope. I remember riding in a small red and black Volkswagen convertible with three other soldiers one Sunday afternoon. As we drove back to the Army base, the driver pulled out a marijuana cigarette and passed it to the two passengers and me. The advice of Daddy quickly flashed in my memory. When the others insisted that I "take a hit," I refused. As they demanded, I asked them to let me out of the car. I knew I could not let Daddy down by going against his advice. I got out of the car and walked back to the Army base. Later when I told Daddy about my experience and that I remembered his direction, he felt terrific that he had taught me well. While fighting as a combat paratrooper in Vietnam, I remembered and followed my daddy's advice on many other occasions. I learned many things from my daddy's teachings and many things from his actions. Frankly, I am still learning from him.

"Behind every great man is a man greater, his father." – Habeeb Akande

Mama: The Humorist

My daddy had a real sense of humor. Many years after I left home, I was elected to the Kansas City, Missouri school board. I visited New York City to appear on the nationally syndicated Donohue Talk Show. Before going to New York, I had done interviews with the Wall Street Journal, New York Times newspaper, and the British Broadcasting Company (BBC), to name a few. The show arranged to pick me up in a long black stretch limousine. The white limo driver pointed out all the amenities in the limo: the entertainment center, the refrigerator with several kinds of drinks, many chips, and candy, and told me I could avail myself of the services. He also told me that I could use the phone in the limo and call anyone I desired. The first person that came to mind was my daddy. I wanted to let him know where I was and what I was doing. I picked up the car phone and called Daddy. I said, *"Daddy, this is your son, Edward. You should see me, I'm riding in a long stretch limo in New York City with a white driver with a black cap, and I decided to use the phone to call and see how you are doing."*

He did not have many questions, but he said, *"Hey can you send me a little something?"* Then followed up with one of his regulars: *"Ahh shit, Mr. Big Time! That'll get it!"* Dad had a way of bringing you back down to earth. He would say one thing when somebody thought they were all of that and a bag of chips*: "Look at that shittin' assed fool, trying to be big, but little is eating his ass up!"* When people would say things to him and try to get on his nerves, he would turn away and say that all you needed to do was *"Hunch yourself and wink your eye at the world!"* I would ask him what that saying meant. He would say, *"It means nothing."*

"The difference between a 'man' and a 'father' is that the former shares his genes, but the latter gives his life." – Craig D. Lounsbrough.

Daddy was no saint, nor did he pretend to be. He started smoking and drinking when he was young, lasting until he was old. He would whip us if we followed his smoking and drinking habits. My mother was pregnant with Robert, my oldest brother, before he married her. He could out-curse a sailor and never made an apology for doing so. At the age of 56, while married to my mother, his lady friend gave birth to a son. Over the past few years, I have had the opportunity to meet and spend a little time with my half-brother, who is the spitting image of my daddy and his daddy. The first time I had an extended talk with my half-brother was when he came to my sister's home, next door to my parents' house. He laughed and carried on similarly to Daddy and had more of Daddy's mannerisms than I do. I have stayed in touch with him over the years. Daddy never said a word to me about his son, but it was well-known throughout the town that the boy was Daddy's son. I never asked Daddy any questions. Daddy had some conversations with a few of my siblings about his son, and some of them developed a closer relationship with him. One of the things that Daddy requested from Robert, my oldest brother, was to please make sure that his son had something to wear to his funeral when he died.

"He who spares his rod hates his son, but he who loves him disciplines him promptly"- Proverbs 13:24

Mama: The Disciplinarian

I have proof that my daddy loved me more than his other children. My evidence comes from the Bible, the word of God. I have known this for a very long time. The Bible passage in Proverbs 13:24 attests to my claim: *"He who spares his rod hates his son, but he who loves him disciplines him promptly."* Let's look at how Daddy demonstrated his greater love for me. When I was just a tiny tot, just starting school, I determined that school was not my place, so I didn't want to go. I was not too fond of the school; maybe, it was because of one of my teachers, Mrs. IMW, who spanked me in front of the class for no reason. I stood at the blackboard trying to find the answer to a math problem. I was wearing short white pants and a short-sleeved white shirt. When I could not complete that complicated problem of *"what came after 1, 2, 3?"* she asked me if I needed help, and I responded, *"yes, ma'am."* She tricked me. I thought she would help me, but instead of helping me, she took a rattan to my skinny little legs. From that moment, I decided that I would never ask for help again for the rest of my life; but more crucially, I would never return to school, no matter the cost.

I stayed in bed the following morning because I developed a stomachache. When Daddy came into the room to get me up for school, I told him I could not go because my stomach was hurting. He told me to show him where it was hurting, and I put my hand on my chest to indicate the place of my pain. He responded, *"boy get yo' little ass in there and get yo'self ready for school!"* When I did not move fast enough for him, he took a belt to my bottom. When Daddy was serious about getting the message across, he would sit down, have you pull your pants down, then tattoo your naked bottom. I was not too fond of that for some strange reason, but I dared not let my disagreement be known.

I knew I needed to develop a better action plan for the next time. I gave some thought to another plot for a couple of days. Bingo! Got it! The night before school, I found two flat head thumb tacks on the dresser. I spent a few minutes thinking about how to pull this off without causing me too much pain. I decided to take one thumb tack and stick it into the heel of my bare foot. I stuck it in more than I had planned, and my little foot started to bleed. Then, I hobbled into the kitchen, where my mother was preparing breakfast, and showed her my bleeding foot. I thought she would have some sympathy for me as she usually did. I knew I had miscalculated when she called Daddy to see what she had quickly diagnosed as a ruse. *"J.D., this boy has stuck a tack in his foot to keep from going to school!"* Daddy examined my foot, asked no questions, ignored the tears rolling down my face, and asked, *"where's my belt?"* Once again, down goes my pants, the burning goes my little legs, and I was crying like a baby, falling to the floor, kicking and scratching like a kitten, Daddy teaching me the lesson of my life. I never tried to pull the wool over my parents' eyes again, at least not like that.

But I still needed to learn my lesson. Sometime later, our pigs got out of the pigpen and went to graze in the cornfield. Daddy sent me to the cornfield to get the pigs to prevent them from destroying the corn crop. I was reluctant to obey but followed his orders without saying a word to let him know I did not want to go and get the pigs. I went up to the field, and just as I expected, the pigs were eating the corn. I attempted half-heartedly to shoo the pigs off, but they continued eating. After a few more futile attempts, I returned to the house and reported to Daddy that I could not get the job done because the pigs had climbed the corn stalks, and I failed to get them to come down. You can imagine what happened to me.

One of my most vital spiritual gifts is martyrdom. I was not aware of that when I was a child. I got more spankings than all my brothers and sisters combined. When I was paying the price with a thrashing for telling a lie or for being mischievous, they were coyly observing the consequences that I was experiencing and deciding not to follow in

my footsteps. Smart! It was not that they did no wrong, but I was always the likely suspect, the proverbial "person of interest." I took a spanking, and they learned a lesson at my expense.
One of the things that I was always confused about when my parents spanked me, was that they would sometimes say, *"this is hurting me more than it's hurting you!"* Daddy did not spare the rod from me! Impossible! I was the one who was getting his "hide-tanned!"

I had other siblings who were mischievous at times, but Daddy was more lenient with them. My second oldest brother, Sterling, comes to mind. A smoking incident at the school, C.H. Hogan Elementary School, involved Sterling and a couple more of our cousins. (The school went as far as the 8th grade in the latter years). The principal, Mrs. VMB, got wind of Sterling and the other boys smoking in the outhouse. I was one of the people she called into her office to investigate whether the allegation was true. I confirmed that the boys were smoking in the toilet. The principal came to our house and told Daddy that his son had been smoking in the toilet at school and suggested that he do something about it so that it would not happen again. Sterling admitted that he had been smoking at school. However, my daddy spared the rod and merely chastised Sterling for his actions. Sterling was probably too old to get a spanking but not too old for Daddy to get in his face. Whenever any of the sons did something that ticked Daddy off, he would say a couple of things: "*Curse me and die!" I brought you into this world, and I can take you out of this world!"*

Again, when I was 17, a short time before I left home to go to the convention in St. Louis with Madear, Daddy had to chastise me for coming in late one night. I had been in a nearby town called Hempstead, a few miles from our home, running around with a boy called "Fox" (a name like that is bound for trouble). Fox had a car, and he did all the driving. He brought me home at about one o'clock in the morning, about an hour past my curfew. I tried to sneak into the house, but that was hard because I had to go inside the house through the living room, where Daddy and Madear always slept. Sure enough, he woke up and said, *"Ina, look at what time this boy is bringing his ass in here, after one o'clock in the morning! Where in the shit have you been this late into the night?"* I told him I had been hanging out with Fox, and his car broke down, making me get home later than I had intended. That experience had no further repercussions, but I felt guilty because I had not told my daddy the complete truth.

Several other times, we said or did something that drew Daddy's ire. Grapes were growing on vines near the road by our house. We (Sterling, Joe, and I) picked the grapes off and decided to make some grape wine. Dad got wind of our plans, took the grape juice, and poured it on the ground. He scolded us but did not spank us. One day the three of us were walking down the road just past our house and saw this little blue and white flat-pack on the ground about half the size of a folded dollar bill. The pack read, "Stand Back," with a smaller print that said, "B.C. Powder." We took a match (why we had a box of matches is a mystery to me now), set the pack afire, and followed the instruction to "Stand Back," ran a short distance away with our hands holding our ears to lessen the impact of the explosion from the pack. There was no explosion. We told Daddy what we had done, and he explained that the Stand Back BC powder was not an explosive device, but a substance taken to relieve arthritis, headaches, and the common cold. He got very tickled at our little episode.

There was an occasion when we played under the willow tree in our backyard and heard a loud voice that said, "Sterling!" To this day, we never determined the source of that voice. We wanted to believe that it was the "voice of God." Fearfully, we ran into the house, closed the door, and peeped out the window. We did not go back outside for the remainder of the day. When Daddy got home, we excitedly told him what we had heard and how we had responded. He pulled us aside and said maybe it was the voice of God and that we had nothing to fear. We were consoled but never heard the voice again, at least not in that manner.

"When a great man dies, for years, the light he leaves behind him lies on the paths of men." – Henry Wadsworth Longfellow.

Mama: Remembered

I was not with Daddy when he died on November 13th, 1995. He was in the hospital, and I had planned to go to Brenham, Texas, to visit him; but my mother informed me there was no need to come at that time because Daddy was feeling much better. I had also planned to attend a school board conference in San Francisco two days later, but I got a call saying that Daddy had died; naturally, I did not go to San Francisco.

I have so many memories of the "Man Called Mama" that time will not permit me to share them all in this document. However, I have tried capturing as many memories as possible. Reading this will give you a better insight into who my daddy was and who he was not. For my family and me, he was a good daddy. For others, maybe Daddy was sometimes a bit imprudent, and he was. Yet, others may have seen him as a philosopher who often spewed wisdom and knowledge wherever he went. For all of us, we will do good to follow his advice: *"Don't take no wooden nickels!"*

"Develop an attitude of gratitude. Say thank you to everyone you meet for everything they do for you." – Brian Tracy.

Daddy, Thank You!
Daddy, thank you for disciplining me the way you did. The fact that I can recall many of these experiences more than 70 years later indicates that I always remembered your teaching. You taught me more about life, family, survival, faith, God, and people than anyone else. You were a genius, wise, intelligent, intellectual, and observant person who impacted the lives of your children, many of your grandchildren, and many others. You never told us that you loved us, but we knew it. You never said you were proud of us, but we felt it. You never asked us to love you, but we will love you forever.

I will always be honored to be called the 5th child of "Mama" and Ina Newsome!

My daddy died on November 13th, 1995, after being hospitalized for three days in Brenham, Texas.

The body of "A Man Called Mama" was buried in the Sample Cemetery, just west of downtown Chappell Hill, about a mile from his one-room barber shop, but his soul rests comfortably in a mansion in heaven with Jesus. May his legacy live on and through each of us daily!

Chapter 6
Joyce M. Newsome-Hargrove

John Douglas Newsome was born on January 7th, 1913. John was an identical twin to James Columbus Newsome, with two older brothers, Artie and Willie, who were born to Phillip and Lottie Newsome. John was called 'Mama,' and James was called "Papa.' They were given these names as little boys. I am not sure by whom or why.

Mama was my daddy. I was the sixth child born to Ina and John. I remember when I was three years old, "yes, three." I was in the way in the kitchen when I was accidentally burned with hot grease (cooking oil), as we call it. Now, I remember it as if it was yesterday. Daddy and Madea took me to the hospital in Bellville, Texas. I can still see the bright lights shining on my face as I lay on the examining table. I remember nothing after that, except that I was blind for five days. While regaining my sight, the first thing I could see was the image of Daddy's old mare, Old Filly.

I was the middle child, with five older and five younger siblings. I was stuck with a lot of washing on the "washboard," as it was called, until the wringer-type washing machines came along. I made homemade starch for their white shirts for church and ironed them all. Yeah, I did most of the work.

Anyway, there were eleven of us. I learned later in the years of one more sibling. You will learn later in my story about the plus one. They seemed pretty busy in those days, thinking we would pick cotton for the rest of our lives. Those were terrible days in the cotton field.

I remember we all got on a huge flatbed truck that took us to the cotton field. We picked cotton all day in the scorching hot sun, ducking and dodging those nasty old cotton worms inching their way all over the cotton leaves, onto our clothes, and all over our cotton sacks. I was probably the only one who was frightened to death of them. On Friday evenings, after slaving all week, the truck would bring us back into town, always stopping at the Buckeyes store. I think it was the only service station at the time. Daddy would buy us a six-cent "cho-cho," the ice cream on a stick, five "jack cookies" for a nickel, and either an orange or strawberry soda water. These were our treats after a long week in the field.

Just a plain ole country guy, Mama Newsome wasn't a man of fancy words. He was not a pretender. He was just a naturally cool guy in his way, and he had his style.

I don't think many knew it, but Daddy had a good singing voice. He could have made it big with training and practice. He often played with a few verses from one of those old hymns. Then he would ask, "How does that sound?" Daddy played around joking sometimes, and when he got tired, he would say, "Ow shit, let me alone!!"

Daddy didn't care about sports; he always said, "Aw hell, if they were playing ball in the backyard, I wouldn't watch 'em!!"

Daddy and Madea gathered us up back when the clowns came to town. I don't remember how many nights they were in Chappell Hill, but it was exciting for us to see the clowns do their magic tricks. It was called the "Uncle Toby" show.

I remember Charles Coates was the first wealthy man I ever heard of in Chappell Hill. He had a large stable for his horses and cows, even buffalo, right up the hill from our house. At a particular time of the year, ole Coates hosted rodeos at the barn and arena. Daddy became excited watching all the cowboys pulling their big trucks and trailers, bringing their horses and cows that would participate in the rodeo.

When night came, Daddy took us to the rodeo. We all sat alone on the fence line watching the cowboys as they performed their acts: barrel racing, what they called cut horses, where the cowboys roped the cows, jumped off the horses, wrestled the cows to the ground, and tied them up with a rope for a certain amount of time, then let them go. That seemed to be the main event of the show, which got Daddy excited. Daddy always said, "The first chance I get, I wanna see the rodeo in Huntsville," but he never got that chance.

Daddy had three horses of his own- Trigger the wild horse, Silver, who was gentler, and at one time, a slow ole mare called Ole Filly.

Daddy had his faults, just as any other human being. Deep down inside, he was a good man. Daddy would say what he wanted to say, and it didn't matter what it was or to whom. Many times, he would use choice words.

Daddy was a hardworking man. He provided for the eleven of us and Madea the best he knew how.

I can imagine him now, back in the day, walking behind the mules and the plow, wiping the sweat from his forehead with his shirt sleeve, never letting go of the plow while breaking the ground for a garden. He planted seeds and vegetables of all kinds. I remember we had to pick and shell lots of peas, snap green beans, and remove the husks from many ears of corn. Such chores were all good when putting meals together, especially when Madea fried fresh corn. It was "oh so good" with the cured ham and bacon from the smokehouse.

I remember the days we had to kill and pick the chickens for cooking. Occasionally, a rabbit was thrown in a skillet with brown gravy, rice, and homemade biscuits. That was when food had a taste. So much for the good ole days. I remember Daddy and the guys bringing the chitterlings into the house in that big number three tub. It was so gross and stinky!! Oh, my lord, I hated hog-killing time.

Daddy and Madea seasoned the fresh meat, then showed us how to grind the meat to make sausage and how to run it through the casing. Daddy had a special little house he called the smokehouse. He seemed proud to hang the sausage, bacon, and hams to smoke and cure for later meals that lasted through the winter. One thing about it, with all the work and preparations, we were never hungry.

We always had what we needed, of course, in those days, you didn't have the option of being choosy. We had what we had, and that was it. No one knew about name-brand shoes or fancy new clothes. I remember wearing the same pair of shoes year-round. When our shoes became loose at the toe, Daddy used this thing called the shoe lass, where he put the shoe on the part shaped like a foot and installed tacks in the toe of the shoe to hold them together. Then they were as good as new. We always dressed nice and clean and looked good, even if we did wear hand-medowns from the white people and from an exceptional person, my fifth-grade teacher, Mrs. Johnson. I remember Madea made shirts for the boys, using her foot-paddling sewing machine. Even now, some people think of us as being 'rich'.

We all had chores, drawing water from the water well, carrying it more than a thousand feet, and splashing water on our feet and the ground. The bucket didn't have much water when we got to the house. The boys had to cut wood and pick up wood chips for the wood-burning heater and the wood-burning stove.

I'm sure Daddy and Madea loved all of us, but you didn't hear them say the word "love'. For whatever reason, Daddy would say at times, "I love all y'all," but never on a one-on-one basis. Daddy and I would argue about things at times that didn't have much meaning. He would soon say, "Aw shit, girl, you don't know anything!!" Mama Newsome was a man who didn't mind telling anyone, "Oh hell, you don't know your asshole from a hole in the ground."

For me, that meant you're dumb. He always had something wild to say; whatever came up came out of his mouth.

One day Daddy and I were talking about being married. This man had the nerve to tell me, "Even if you were getting your ass whipped, you should have stayed there anyway." I quickly let him know he was living in the wrong world. Most conversations between us were off the chain. I am talking about a man that never lifted one finger toward my mother, nor did he ever threaten her.

One day I said something that struck a nerve. He sat there with a smirk on his face, batting his eyes fast. On my way out the door, he shouted, "It's a wonder the flies ain't following your ass."

Mama Newsome was a good man. He talked a lot of crap, usually meaning what he said. He would tell you quickly; I ain't giving you "nare" damn red cent. Nope, he wasn't giving you, his money. He always said if you make a quarter, you should be able to save a dime. He probably could because he meant what he said, not one red cent. Well, not to me, anyway.

Daddy didn't mind letting you know how he felt. Of course, I never let his off-the-wall talk hurt my feelings, even when he said, "Robert Lee got more sense than all of y'all put together." Robert was our oldest brother. I don't remember the conversation that day, but we were all in the yard. He always had us in the yard doing something, whether it was cutting brush or moving trash.

One day he had us cutting a path through the bushes by the house. I looked up, and he was standing there with a silly grin on his face. He was holding a very tall stick, wearing his hat, undershirt, and pants, of course, being eaten by mosquitoes, saying, "Do I look like Moses in the wilderness?" He thought it was funny.

Daddy loved his dogs. Dover was a Dobermann Pinscher, and Rover was a German Shepherd. He kept them inside the front yard fence because he thought they were awful. One day, a good friend named John was visiting. This was when Daddy discovered the dogs were "all bark." He said to John, "Man shit, they will eat your ass up if you go inside that fence!!" John replied, "Okay, watch this." John walked closer to the fence where the bad dogs were. He made eye contact with the dogs, and after staring at them for a second, the dogs whimpered and sat back on their hind legs. Daddy was speechless. He soon responded, "Aw shit, man, I didn't know that." So much for the bad dogs.

I think Daddy thought I was a handy person. Whenever the water well or air conditioner stopped working, I was called to clean the fire ants off the relay switch to get them started again. That was until the problem was too big for me to fix.

He sat and watched me cut the plantation using a push mower, saying, "Girl shit, it didn't take you long either!!" Yeah, right. He would not say I did a good job.

Daddy had his style of everything, clothes, words, facial expressions, and thoughts. I used to hear him say, "Never let your left hand know what your right hand is doing." To me, this meant don't tell all your business to everybody, and everybody doesn't need to know what you do.

As I said, his style was his starched ironed white shirt daily, suspenders, and wide-leg slacks with the cuff. He never owned a pair of sneakers. He always wore boots or his Stacey Adams. Daddy was sometimes referred to as the "rich man." Even now, some of the Polish people that grew up around him still refer to Daddy as the rich man, the big shot, or as he would say, the "Big shit!!"

Daddy was afraid of the city. As a matter of fact, he did not like to drive himself just nine miles to Brenham to get his own medicine. I don't remember the occasion, but I drove to Luby's restaurant down highway 290 with him riding in the truck's front seat one day. He held onto the dashboard for dear life, complaining, "Too damn many cars for me." As soon as we finished our meal with the rest of the family, he looked strange, saying, "Shit girl, let's get out of here." I could not get him back to Chappell Hill fast enough.

Mama Newsome was quite a character. He could fry good chicken. He always said the trick to frying good chicken is to fry it in nice and slow oil. One day he fired up the BBQ pit to cook some meat. When the meat was cooked, he told me to taste it. Of course, I knew it was not chicken. I asked, "What is that?" He replied "It's Armadillo." "Oh no," I said, "I'm not tasting that." "Aw shit girl, taste the thing!" He got fighting mad because I wouldn't eat it, saying, "Shit, you don't know what's good!"

Memories, memories, memories. I remember when we used to go down the road in the woods, across the crumbly creepy bridge, around a corner, and crawl under a barbed wire fence to pick pecans in the cold. It was too cold to be under all those pecan trees. We picked enough to sell, but now that I think about it, I don't remember getting my share of the money.

The Case of the Rolling Truck

One day Daddy came home. As he would say, he had been hanging out "up the road." The edge of the road was under the big tree in the front yard. We were all in the yard, including big Wayne and Marvin. These two visited often. We looked up in time to see the truck as it began to roll, headed for the road. Madea took off running, intending to jump in the truck to stop it. Daddy shouted out to her, "Ina, let the bastard roll! Let it roll!!" Wayne and Marvin could not stop laughing. Daddy looked at them, cussing, "What the shit y'all laughing at fellows?"

Home in 1972

During the summer of 1972, things were not going well with my first husband and me. I separated myself and my two girls from that abusive marriage. I don't remember the exact date, but I rode the Greyhound bus from Houston to Chappell Hill. Daddy was hanging out at the store where the ole timers went for entertainment, drinking beer, lying, whatever else they did. I asked him to drive me to the house. Of course, he was not happy about leaving the crowd. At the store I learned about our plus-one brother from another mother. I was darned hot with him then, so later, I threatened to tell Madea what I was told. He threatened to burst my teeth out if I opened my mouth. That surprised me because Daddy was not that type of person, but after that ordeal and knowing about that situation, I guess I lost a little respect for him for a while, especially coming out of my situation. It was somewhat hard to listen to anything he had to say.

I started working at Maddox Furniture. I met one of the company's drivers and we started dating. Daddy was unhappy when he learned I was going on trips with him. He warned me to stop traveling with him, but guess what? The more he told me not to, the faster I jumped on board. After all, I was a grown-ass woman in her early 20s.

Daddy pretended to be as mean as a junkyard dog, but he wasn't. He liked to fuss and talked a lot of smack, but his bark was bigger than his bite. His ways were his ways, whether you liked them or not.

When it came to stormy weather, he was a real scaredy cat. Daddy got nervous at the roar of thunder and lightning flashing across the sky. He wanted everyone to sit still and be quiet. My baby sister got in trouble chewing and popping her gum. He would hold his hand to her mouth for her to spit the gum out.

A few years later, I had my own house built. Since my house was brick, he thought he would be safer when the storms would pop up, so he came to my house. Madea always told Daddy when God gets ready for you it doesn't matter where you are. But that never stopped him from running to my house for cover.

Mama had his special recliner in the corner of the living room, where he could see out of the window, up the road, and around the corner. He wanted to see everything going and coming. He would get upset when we put up the Christmas tree, complaining that he couldn't see anything.

As I stated previously, Mama Newsome was a good man. He had his faults like everyone else on Earth, and yes, he used words that some people thought were inappropriate, but some of the words are in the Bible. If you would search your Bible, you will find that the word "**BASTARD"** is in Deuteronomy 23:2. In Mark 23:14, the word **"DAMNED"** is mentioned. Daddy's main word was **"SHIT."** Well, that's just another word for poop. **"HELL"** is found in Mark 9:43, and I imagine it is in many other places. So much for what is called cuss words.

Daddy got so angry with me one day. He planned to kill a goose for Madea to cook. Far out in the yard, with the goose's neck stretched across a log of wood, he called my two oldest daughters to bring the ax to cut the goose's head off. I heard him say, "Cut the damn thing!"

I got there just in time to stop them. Those poor kids were terrified. Both of them ran as fast as they could to the house.

Leaving the house one day, he wanted to know where I was going. I replied, "I have a CPR class to go to." Guess what he said, "Aw shit, that little nickel's worth of CPR ain't gonna save nobody." And guess what? On Saturday, November 11th, 1995, Madea called for me and my girls to come and help get him off the floor. With the help of my son-in-law-to-be, we managed to stretch him out on the couch, and I had to use the nickel's worth of CPR I learned to breathe for him. While being coached by the paramedics over the phone, I kept him safe until they arrived. Daddy was transported to the hospital by EMS. In those days, we could camp out in the waiting room, and camp out we did. We all stayed in the waiting room for the few days Daddy was alive. Daddy had been unresponsive during the first night in the hospital. Early Monday morning Clarence and I arrived to visit him. He rose from his pillow, and called Clarence's name out loud, shocking everyone in the room. As the day went by, he continued to have visitors in and out, not knowing who was there. On the third day, we continued to surround him, with Madea standing calmly at the head of his bed, talking to him.

I remember during the day, he asked for ice cream. I am unsure what kind he was given, but he got what he requested.

The day continued with all of us at his side; then night fell, with all of us at his bed, and with him looking up as the death angels were all around. I don't know how to describe the feeling and the sight of him taking his last breath on Earth. Oh my God, what an experience to encounter. "A Man Called Mama" went to be with the Lord on November 13th, 1995.

Chapter 7
Travis Newsome

1 The Lord is my light and my salvation; whom shall I fear? the Lord is the strength of my life; of whom shall I be afraid?

2 When the wicked, even mine enemies and my foes, came upon me to eat up my flesh, they stumbled and fell.

3 Though a host should encamp against me, my heart shall not fear: though war should rise against me, in this will I be confident.

4 One thing have I desired of the Lord, that will I seek after; that I may dwell in the house of the Lord all the days of my life, to behold the beauty of the Lord, and to enquire in his temple.

5 For in the time of trouble He shall hide me in his pavilion: in the secret of his tabernacle shall He hide me; He shall set me up upon a rock.

6 And now shall mine head be lifted up above mine enemies round about me: therefore, will I offer in his tabernacle sacrifices of joy; I will sing, yea, I will sing praises unto the Lord.

7 Hear, O Lord, when I cry with my voice: have mercy also upon me, and answer me.

8 When Thou saidst, seek ye my face; my heart said unto Thee, Thy face, Lord, will I seek.

9 Hide not thy face far from me; put not thy servant away in anger: thou hast been my help; leave me not, neither forsake me, O God of my salvation.

10 When my father and my mother forsake me, then the Lord will take me up.

11 Teach me thy way, O Lord, and lead me in a plain path, because of mine enemies.

12 Deliver me not over unto the will of my enemies: for false witnesses are risen up against me, and such as breathe out cruelty.

13 I had fainted, unless I had believed to see the goodness of the Lord in the land of the living.

14 Wait on the Lord: be of good courage, and he shall strengthen thine heart: wait, I say, on the Lord.

(Psalm 27:1-14, KJV)

Daddy would fluently recite Psalm 27 from memory. It was pretty impressive to hear him do it, and when he did, there was absolute silence in his presence. There was something special about how he did it. The gruffness, which was pretty much his normal voice, was not there. His head was always slightly bowed. Immediately afterward, everything would return to normal, and one of his favorite words would be heard rolling off that same tongue and lips. Daddy was quite a character, very smart, but also very funny, although he never cracked jokes.

I was the 7th child born to Daddy and our mother, Ina. Yes, 7th - so much for perfection and completion, as after me, Jerry, John, Delores, and Oscar were born. My experiences with Daddy were different from most of my other siblings. I was the first of the eight boys to stop working in the fields. That was because when I started high school, I had to stay after school for athletic practices. I am not sure why Daddy allowed it because he cared nothing about sports, absolutely nothing. Jerry and John, chapters 8 and 9, were left to work the fields.

I don't remember a lot of things about my very early life, but there are a couple of things I do remember. I was probably 4 or 5 years old when a knot appeared on my right inner leg a few inches above the knee. I remember Mudear and Daddy taking me to Bellville to see a doctor. When we got there, I remember Daddy saying, 'Ina, take him in, and I will stay in the car.' I never asked Daddy why he remained in the car but never really thought about it. I was just a little kid. The knot was lanced. A slightly raised scar remains on my leg today. As I reflect back on that day and the distinct smell of the cold doctor's office, I bet Daddy stayed in the car to pray. My parents had a strong faith, as displayed in their prayer life and reading of the Bible. Apparently, the knot was benign. I've had no issue with it since. I doubt it was tested anyway.

I was told that I helped Daddy build our home back in 1953 or 54. I am pretty sure it was nothing more than holding a board or retrieving a hammer or some other tool. All of my older siblings were home during that time, so I am not sure why I would have held that role, but I am taking credit for helping anyway. I'm kinda thinking I may have been the architect.

Daddy was a source of pride, and it was shown in almost everything he did. He smoked King Edward cigars and wore white shirts. I was told by my siblings that at one time, he smoked cigarettes, but I don't remember. I never saw my father in jeans or short pants or a shirt other than the color white. I am pretty sure he did not own a belt because all I remember were black suspenders. The white shirt/suspenders were his signature.

As you can probably imagine, he was quite a disciplinarian. I don't recall any of my older siblings disagreeing with him the least bit. We did what he asked us to do and did it without complaining. We knew better than to complain. Speaking of discipline, I grew up in an era where the rod was not spared, but I remember only one "beating" from Daddy. Not sure of my age, but Daddy accused me and Jerry (Chapter 8) of trying to burn down the house. I think we had been playing with matches, but I know we were not trying to burn down the house. That made no sense. I always thought Daddy had plenty of common sense, and he did, but this made no sense. I think I am still sore. That was the only whipping I remember from Daddy.

I remember when he came home in a 1956 red and white Chevrolet and, a few years later, a blue 1959 Chevrolet. How could we afford those cars? I remember how proud he was and how excited the entire family was about a new car, albeit pre-owned. We probably had the newest car in town among black families. There was always a special sense of pride as it related to the new cars. The pride was unique, but nothing nor anyone impressed Daddy. That is just who he was.

Another special time of the year was when we sold our only bale of cotton for the season to the Chappell Hill, Texas cotton gin. I remember it was always a struggle trying to get a complete bale, but we all were excited and many of us accompanied the trailer containing the cotton to the gin when we did. Although it was not compressed, we called it a bale. It was a wagon of roughly 8x5x6 full of freshly picked cotton. That was the product we took to the gin. When we were not picking our own cotton, we would pick the cotton of others in the area to help support the family. Daddy rarely worked in the fields with my generation. He made us do most of the work. Daddy instilled a strong work ethic and a sense of entrepreneurship by making us work hard and showing us how to earn money. He would wake us up early in the morning. I still remember the dew from those early mornings. Entrepreneurship apparently took hold because not one of Daddy's eight boys has ever held a corporate job. I am not really sure what Daddy was doing when we were working in the field, probably making another baby.

Not only was Daddy a farmer but also a barber. He did not become a barber because of the number of boys in the family. It was always a part of his plan. He was cutting hair even before the birth of our oldest sibling, Robert. Daddy never had formal training to be a barber which also means there was no license to cut hair. His dilapidated barbershop was one-half block off Main Street, in downtown Chappell Hill. He was never questioned or bothered by the authorities. And no, the authorities were not on the take. Daddy was not that kind of person. Everyone knew he was there. I really don't know how that building stood in that condition all those years. Daddy never paid any income taxes on his hair cutting earnings or his earnings from farming. I never ever heard him talking about having to file his taxes and getting a tax refund. This was an oxymoron because Daddy's record keeping was impeccable and continuous during his entire hair cutting career.

We think having a lot of kids facilitated his absence from the field, and the kids were his retirement plan, his 401 J. D. and Ina-K. It paid off. Our parents, later in life, never had a desire for something that they did not receive, which included the kids building two brand new homes - one in 1968 (Robert, Sterling, Joe, and Edward), where we enjoyed electricity, indoor plumbing, and central air for the first time, and a second home that was all-brick in 1987, with Jerry and me being added to the previous four siblings mentioned. It is impossible to describe the pride displayed about what "the boys" had done. I am not sure if my sisters financially participated in the building of the house in 1987 but surely not in 1968. Daddy had always wanted a brick home because he was so afraid of tornadoes and hurricanes. I don't recall a tornado ever visiting Chappell Hill, but I will never forget Hurricane Carla in September of 1961, a couple of months before my 12th birthday. That was the only time in my life that I knew for a fact that Daddy was afraid. If you could see the house we lived in at that time, you would definitely understand.

Another special time of the year was in the fall when it was time to kill a hog. That was exciting because it provided several types of meat and treats. Although the hog killing time was exciting, it was also part of the reason why we never went without food on the table. We never went to bed hungry.

I have no idea how my parents came up with our names, but they apparently had an affinity for the letter "J." I think it was because Daddy's first name was John, and his twin brother was James. Five of my ten siblings' names start with "J." They are Johnnie, Joe, Joyce, Jerry, and John. Perhaps they should have stuck with the J's because there was some confusion about my name. I was told from the beginning that my name was Travis Douglas Lee Newsome. The Douglas came from Daddy because I was told he wanted me to have his middle name. Robert, my oldest brother's middle name was Lee. He wanted in on my name. When I was old enough to understand, I loved my name and was quite pleased with it because had my other older siblings gotten into the act, my name would have been Travis Douglas Lee May Gene James Marie Newsome. I learned in 1971 that my birth certificate had to be corrected because it showed me having Daddy's first two names plus Robert's middle name, which means the name shown on my birth certificate was John Douglas Lee Newsome. The corrected birth certificate showed only Travis Newsome without me having a middle name. I asked Daddy what happened but he nor my mother had an answer. I now love having just a first and last name. The sad truth is from my date of birth, November 28, 1949 until July 26, 1971, my name was John Douglas Lee Newsome. I only became Travis Newsome when the birth certificate was corrected on July 27, 1971. Someone was really confused not just because of my name but also because the birth certificates said there were 5 additional children that were living. I am the seventh child and all of my older siblings were still living at the time.

Daddy was the only left-handed person in the family.

Twin- Daddy was a twin, no twin found anywhere else in the family.

How he treated our mother - I never heard Daddy raise his voice at our mother. Now, don't get me wrong, I had heard him raise his voice but it was always at one of us. I never saw him hug or kiss her. He never bought her flowers or gifts. I never heard him tell my mother that he loved her. I recently saw a photo with his arm around her.

How did Daddy feel about:

Praise- Daddy was not big on praise. He did not praise and did not expect praise. I don't ever recall Daddy saying something as simple as, "Thank you." I don't ever remember him asking, "And what do you say" to someone or to a sibling to whom he had given something. Don't get me wrong, Daddy was not a mean person. He was kind and caring and a great provider, but as far as affection was concerned, he was terrible. He had none. I don't recall ever receiving or giving my father a hug. If you would ask Daddy, "Do you love me?" -without hesitating, he would say, "I love all y'all."

The Afro Hair Style- I will never forget when I came home for Christmas after my first semester at Oklahoma University with an afro in 1969. He did not like it at all and thought people that wore them were ignorant. He said so. Daddy was a barber, so I guess his feelings may have been a little jaded about men wearing long hair. He offered to give me a haircut, but I explained this was the style now and all the black students at Oklahoma wore their hair that way so he let me slide. (I am not going to say what he said should be done with style but he did suggest it should be covered with something.)

Sports - I think I saw Daddy throw a homemade softball once. I never saw him play catch with any of my siblings or play with me or any of them in any way. He never purchased sports equipment for any of us, to my knowledge. He never purchased anything for any of us. There is one exception though. I am aware of him shopping for a small toy at J. C. Penney's in Brenham (10 miles west of Chappell Hill) because I saw him pick up and put down a couple of small toys. He did not see me because I immediately darted out of the store. This was during my Christmas break of 1971. I could not figure out why he would be purchasing a small toy only to surmise later it was probably for Early, who was born just over two years earlier. Who is Early? He is Daddy's "outside child," a son by another mother who resembles Daddy ten times more than any of his other sons. I never had a conversation with Daddy about Early, and to my knowledge, no one else did either, except maybe my oldest brother Robert. More about Early later.

Daddy said if the World Series was in the backyard, he would not attend. Daddy had no interest in sports, PERIOD. I am pretty sure he did not understand the magnitude of my full Track scholarship to Oklahoma University. I don't recall him congratulating me, even before the scholarship. Daddy never attended any of my sporting events at Brenham High School, even though I was a star athlete, lettering in 4 sports and becoming the first Black athlete at many things at Brenham High. Sports just did not interest him. I did not tell him about me winning conference championships at Oklahoma. I told Mudear everything and I have no idea if she shared those details with Daddy. If she did, he never said anything to me about it. When he found out that I had been chosen to visit 8 countries in Africa and also Israel in 1972, he thought that was nice. He always had a desire but I don't think it was a real strong desire to go to the Holy Land. He sounded a little bit happy for me that I was going.

Dominoes - Daddy was not much of a domino player but he and our mother taught us how to play the game. He did not spend as much time playing the game with us as our mother nor was, he as good of a player as she was. My sister Joyce told me she, Daddy and Mudear played frequently but Daddy was not very good and occasionally would throw the dominoes on the floor if he did not like his domino hand. I am so happy I never picked up such a habit when learning and playing the game.

Bell Bottom Jeans - Clown paints, and just like the afro, people that wore such jeans were ignorant. Remember, we are talking about a man that never wore a pair of jeans.

Mourner's Bench- (the front row/bench at church reserved during revival for those seeking the Lord to be saved). Daddy did not believe children should seek Christ and become Christians before the age of 12, That was pretty much the sentiment of every adult or parent in Chappell Hill. The belief was that children simply didn't understand what they were doing. So, each summer, there was a two-week revival so kids that were at least 12 and kids that had not gotten religion the previous year(s) could get religion, be baptized, and join a church. It was also the belief that, for some reason, if you did and did not have religion by the age of 13 or thereafter, you would go to Hell if you died. As a result, all 11 siblings went to the mourner's bench the summer after their 12th birthday. For me, that was July 1962. I accepted Christ on July 12th, 1962. Both parents were pleased and satisfied that I had found Jesus as my Savior.

Birds and the Bees and "Me Too" -Daddy never talked to me about the "birds and the bees," and he did not talk to any of my siblings either, to the best of my knowledge. Perhaps he thought because a new baby was showing up every two years, we would figure out where they came from. I never heard Daddy mention the word sex or anything relating to sex which is probably the reason I did not talk to him, my mother, or anyone when I was molested by the sitting minister of our local St. John A.M.E. church in the summer of 1963 after riding with him to visit a church in Sauney Stand, Texas after the morning service at St. John. On our return to Chappell Hill, he asked me if I wanted to drive. It was not uncommon for very young country farm kids to be driving at the age of 12 or so. Of course, I wanted to drive and I said yes. As I was driving, he placed his hand between my legs. I was so embarrassed and ashamed. Although I have been beyond that for years, I find it difficult to write about today. After that, I never came within 10 feet of that man again although I attended church every Sunday. I often wondered if he molested anyone else because I am aware of a couple of my classmates making trips with him and some more than once. If I would have spoken to Daddy about it, I probably could have prevented him from molesting other young boys.

I do remember Daddy asking me about the young lady that accused me of being the father of her child and asking me what I was going to do. I explained to Daddy that I was not that child's father and further explained that during the Christmas break of 1971, I did have a date with the young lady who I dated in high school, which resulted in some bad behavior. I know the exact date because the next day I had to leave to return to the University of Oklahoma. Well almost 11 months later, ten months and 20 days to be exact, (46 weeks and three days) a baby was born. Daddy, I am not the baby's daddy. I can hear Maury saying, "YOU ARE NOT THE FATHER." Daddy did not have any more questions.

Knowing now what I did not know at the time, Daddy had stepped outside of his marriage and fathered his 12th child, Early Kemp, a couple of years earlier. That would explain him shopping for a toy a year earlier in Brenham. I understand he was providing some assistance which probably prompted his question to me about the aforementioned child. During my last two years of high school, I would see this lady sitting in Daddy's truck with him outside of Black Hawk's joint (a shabby little beer and chips place). Daddy never would go inside the place, and many times he would sit in his truck by himself. On more than two occasions, I saw her in Daddy's truck, but I never said a word. I was ashamed and embarrassed because it was pretty obvious something was going on. Everyone in Chappell Hill knew it. Daddy could not deny being the father, even if he wanted to do so. I wonder if he ever thought about pinning it on his identical twin brother. Did they ever discuss it? The answer is no because Daddy was always good at taking care of his responsibilities, including his mistakes. I am relatively certain the DNA would have worked in his favor. But get this, Early looks ten times more like Daddy than any of his other 11 children. If Early were placed in a lineup with his 11 half-siblings, 100 out of 100 people would have picked him as Daddy's child over the rest of us.

I often wonder if I should have confronted Daddy or said something to my mother or siblings about this when I saw this lady in his truck, but I never had the courage.

Irregardless - Daddy hated this word, and so do I, and yes, I did say word, because it is.

Is irregardless a word? Let's ask Merriam Webster. Irregardless was popularized in dialectal American speech in the early 20th century. Its increasingly widespread spoken use called it to the attention of usage commentators as early as 1927. The most frequently repeated remark about it is that "there is no such word." There is such a word, however. It is still used primarily in speech, although it can be found from time to time in edited prose. Its reputation has not risen over the years, and it is still a long way from general acceptance. Use *regardless* instead.

On Saturday, November 11th, 1995, while attending a Blue Cross Blue Shield of Kansas City board of directors meeting in San Diego, California, I received a phone call at my hotel which informed me that Daddy had been admitted to the hospital. There was no immediate information on his condition. I lost my appetite that evening. The next day, the board attended a San Diego Chargers Kansas City Chiefs football game that Kansas City won. It was difficult for me to get excited. I still did not have much of an appetite. Dinner had been planned at a nice fancy restaurant as usual for the evening. It is impossible for me to describe the very unusual feeling that covered my entire body after the phone call came through that Sunday evening. I was numb. I had never felt that way before and I have never felt that way again. It was not a good feeling. We flew home that Sunday night and when I called Texas on Monday morning to learn of Daddy's condition, I was told there was some improvement and that he wanted ice cream. That was his last meal because later in the evening after Robert arrived, (his favorite son) he took a turn for the worst and succumbed to his illness on November 13th, 1995. Mama Newsome was no more.

His funeral was a few days later.

I dedicated a poem to him. Thank you, Daddy, for everything.

Chapter 8
Jerry E. Newsome

I am Jerry Ennis Newsome, the eighth child of John Douglas and Ina Newsome. I was born January 20th in Chappell Hill, Texas. My fraternal grandparents were Phillip and Lottie Newsome. They had four sons, who were named Artie, Willie, James, & John Newsome. James and John were identical twins. For reasons unknown to me, James and John were nicknamed "Papa & Mama." My father was "Mama."

My grandmother Lottie Newsome moved to Fort Worth, Texas in the mid 1950's to work as a maid for a white lady named Mrs. Nance. She was able to work hard and long enough to purchase 30 acres of land in Chappell Hill, Texas. She later moved back home, to live on the land her hard work had purchased. Dad (Mama) stayed in Chappell Hill as an adult, to work and farm the land. My three uncles relocated to Houston and other places to work other jobs. My parents had 11 children, who were named Robert, Johnnie, Sterling, Joe, Edward, Joyce, Travis, Jerry, John, Delores, and Oscar. Dad was short in stature with a 3rd grade education but was very tall in wisdom and common sense. Daddy (Mama) was a farmer and a barber. My mother, Ina, helped on the farm and later worked in the school system as a chef. Madea, which we called her, was about 5'9", and was very wise and smart also, with a 10th grade education.

Daddy had a barber shop in downtown Chappell Hill where he would cut hair on Saturdays. He would leave early in the morning and return home in the evening. Madea would go to the local grocery store (Stanley's) to buy groceries on credit and Daddy would stop by there on his way home to pay for the groceries. I remember when he came home fussing because the bill was so high. The grocery bill was $7.00 for the week. The groceries would consist of items such as certain staples, like salt, sugar, flour, baking powder, syrup, and some meat. Our mother had a garden where most of the vegetables came from. On the farm we raised hogs and chickens. In the late fall, we would slaughter a hog, salt most of it down and hang the meat in the smoke house. The salt would cure the meat; therefore, there was no need for a refrigerator, which was a good thing, because we did not have one or electricity for that matter. We had wood stoves, heaters, and kerosene lamps.

Daddy (Mama), as I said earlier, was a man with a lot of wisdom. Daddy had many quotes and famous sayings. Not all of them were suited for your children or something one would say in the local church.

A few of them are:

"Look at him, want to be big, but little is eating his ass up." (This is someone who wanted to be a big shot).

"Hunch yourself and wink your eye at the world." (Pretend or try to fool someone).

"Boy if you keep doing what you are doing, you will never have anything as long as your ass hole points toward the ground."

"An opinion is like an ass hole, everybody got one."

"I would not go to a shitting-ass world series baseball game if it was out in the backyard." (He hated sports)

"Chew now and swallow later; all I want to see is elbows and assholes." (This referred to picking cotton).

"It is so quiet you can hear a rat piss on cotton."

"Water is water, fire is fire, where there is a dollar bill, every man is a liar."

Daddy (Mama Newsome) was a different or somewhat fun person. Some of the things he would say and do would humor just about anyone.

He did not have a finance degree or much formal education, but he knew about money and was able to manage it. He would say "Don't spend everything you got, save some." This was his way of teaching budgeting. He was never broke. When he died in November of 1995, he had a hundred-dollar bill in his wallet. Dad would say, "Send me some so I can have a little some in my pocket."

While working on the house or on the truck or just doing something using his hands, he would say, "Aw shit, that ah do, it is better than it was."

Daddy belonged to the Baptist church (Ebenezer Missionary Baptist Church) and my mother belonged to the Methodist church (Saint John African Methodist Church). The Baptist Church would have service only on the first and third Sundays whereas the Methodist Church would have service every Sunday. All of my siblings would go to church with our mother. I don't recall us ever going to church with Daddy. Sometimes my mother's pastor, Pastor Eath would stop by on Sunday after church. Dad likes to argue with preachers and talk stuff. He said to Pastor Eath, "Eath, would you say what I say?" I don't remember his answer, but Dad would start cussing to see if the pastor would repeat what he said. He did not.

We lived in the country in a small frame house that was built on blocks in the early days of growing up in the country. The house did not have indoor plumbing, nor a central heating system or electricity. It did not get very cold in the winter but got very hot in the summer. Our source of heat was a wood heater. We drew water from a well, and we used kerosene for light. We had an outhouse (outdoor toilet). The next house that I can remember was built in 1969 and did have running water and electricity. I think it also had an indoor bathroom. We picked cotton and corn, and raised hogs. There was not much else for extracurricular activities.

We started driving at early ages; between the ages of 5 and 10. Daddy would fuss about Sterling driving. People would snitch on him and tell Dad that they saw him driving very fast. Therefore, this would limit our driving time. Daddy would say, "I ain't goanna let y'all tear up this car like Sterling did the other one. I remember several cars that we had when I was home. I remember the red and white 1956 Chevrolet Bel Air 4 door sedan, the 1959 Chevrolet Bel Air 4 door sedan, and the blue and white 1964 Chevrolet Bel Air 4 door sedan. After I moved to Kansas City in 1973, we bought our parents a new 1974 Chevrolet Nova. In later years, Daddy would start driving trucks. My mother wrecked the 1959 Chevrolet, and it was several months before we got another car. During that interim period, our mode of transportation was a horse. We would ride the horse to the store and to other places, or we would walk. After that period, Daddy went to the bank to borrow some money to purchase the 1964 Chevrolet. I don't remember much conversation about the car being wrecked.

Daddy always wore a white shirt, suspenders, Stacy Adams shoes and a hat. He did not ever wear tennis shoes, or short pants. He kept pens or pencils in his shirt pocket pencil holder. Daddy was afraid of bad weather; when storms were raging, with thunder and lighting, he would get very quiet. He would make us be quiet because 'God was working.' I recall seeing him sometimes, looking out of the window and saying, "Lord help Jesus."

Daddy did not do a lot of driving, especially out of town. When there was an occasion or reason to go to Houston (about 60 miles away) he would get our cousin, Sandy Newsome, to drive us. Driving on the highway would make Daddy very nervous.

I did not get a chance to spend much one-on-one time with my daddy. There was no talk about the birds and bees, there was no "I love you." I do remember him showing me how to install brakes on a truck. Daddy did not do any illegal drugs. He used to drink, smoke cigars, chew tobacco, and dip snuff. One day he came home fussing at me saying "Boy I heard that you were on that stuff." (marijuana) As of now, I have never smoked marijuana in my 71 plus years of living. I don't know where he got that from or who told him that. Daddy taught us the best he could, based on what he knew. Daddy was not a mean man; He was a great father who tried to keep us in line. I think he did a great job. He was probably more on the conservative side when it came to politics and religion. However, he did not think much of right-wing conservative radio talk shows which I will refrain from naming.

Travis was particularly good in sports in high school, he lettered in four sports and had to spend a lot of time after school practicing sports. Daddy didn't like sports and I don't remember him ever attending sporting events. I could only run track because I had to come home after school to work. After he saw what Travis had done, our sporting events were limited.

Daddy was considered a great street philosopher. People would sit around to listen and argue with him. He was not afraid to express his opinion or tell you where to go.

Without any formal training, Dad was a barber, a farmer, a mechanic, and a carpenter. I have learned to do most of these things just by watching him.

As far as punishments went, we did not ever get spankings; we got whippings. We did not get away with much of anything. My mother did most of the whippings, however, Daddy once saw some matches that had been struck outside of the house and decided to whip Travis and me without any questions. He made the assumption that Travis and I had tried to set the house on fire. John was sleeping at the time, but it turned out that it was he who had struck the matches. When

John woke up, Dad said, "Ina (mother) should I whip John?" John did not get a whipping.

Living in the country and not having much, we were considered poor, because not much money was available. They were able to make things work, though, and we did not go hungry. In the summer times we picked cotton for some Polish people in the area for money to help with the household income. On Saturdays we (the children) were able to keep all the money we made to buy our school clothes. Other things we did for money were picking dewberries and selling them on the side of the highway, as well as picking pecans (from a nearby landowner's property, so we'd get to keep half to sell) and selling them to the local grocery store. We were taught to do what it takes to survive. School started in September; however, we did not start school full time for the year until October or November because it was still cotton-picking season. We did get a chance to go to school if it rained.

I left home on August 20th of 1973 (which was my youngest sister Delores' birthday) and drove my 1957 Chevy to Kansas City, Missouri with my baby brother Oscar.

Daddy was very proud of his children, but he did not have many ways of expressing it. He would be happy to see us coming back home during the summer or just any time. We loved our parents and did as much as we could for them while they were living; we sent them money, bought them cars, built them houses, and did things just because. The last house we built was a brick house, it had two bedrooms, one bath, central heating and air, indoor plumbing, and a carport. He would brag about us among some of his associates. He did not consider people as friends.

These are just some of the memories that I have about Daddy (Mama Newsome) while living in Chappell Hill, Texas and Kansas City, Missouri.

My daddy (Mama Newsome) died on November 13th 1995 and his twin brother (Papa Newsome) died on his birthday on January 7th 1975. Uncle Willie B died on October 18th, 1992, and Uncle Artie died on July 22nd, 1996. These were the four sons of Phillip and Lottie Newsome.

My Bio

Jerry Ennis Newsome, the 8th child of John D. and Ina Newsome was born January 20th, 1952, in Chappell Hill, Texas. Jerry attended Chappell Hill Elementary School until the sixth grade; Alton Junior High for the 7th and 8th, graduated from Brenham High School in June of 1971, and graduated from Blinn Junior College in June of 1973. Jerry then moved to Kansas City, Missouri in August of 1973. He graduated in 1980 from the University of Missouri in Kansas City with a BA in

Business Administration. Jerry has been working as a full time Real Estate Appraiser since 1977. He has no plans to retire. He loves traveling to different countries, mostly African countries. He has traveled to Israel, Brazil, Kenya, Ethiopia, Ghana, Morocco, Greece, Egypt, Grenada, Mexico, the Dominican Republic, Canada, and several other Caribbean countries. He has gone on several missionary trips in Brazil, Guinea, Ethiopia, and near his home, in the Kansas City area. He is one of the founding members of the United Believers Community Church. Jerry is currently married to Rosalind L. McGee. He has a total of 5 children; Kelly Newsome of New York, Austin Newsome of Kansas City, Missouri, Jamie Newsome of Portland, Oregon, Anthony Newsome of Kansas City, Missouri, and Mercedes McGee-Williams of Detroit, Michigan. He has been playing professional dominos since 1978; Jerry and his brother Robert won the World Championship Domino Tournament in the doubles division in 1995.

Chapter 9
John D. Newsome

I lived with my mother and father for 18 years, in a small town called Chappell Hill, Texas. My father was always consistent. He had the same personality all his life. He was the type of person that would not bite his tongue, always telling it like it was.

My father's real name was John Douglas Newsome, and my name is John Daniel Newsome. I remember him jokingly saying, 'I don't want no shittin' ass Junior!' and that was fine with me. Pretty much everyone in the small town knew him as Mama Newsome. I really never knew exactly why he was called Mama, and I hadn't ever really thought about it. I kind of assumed it was because my father liked to cook. As you read this book, you may find out from some of my other siblings.

My father had an identical twin brother, who they called Papa Newsome. How he got that nickname, I really don't know. My father went to a Baptist church, and my mother went to a Methodist church. You could hear my father praying out loud every morning if you were awake.

I remember my father would always wear white shirts, regardless of what he was doing. Whether working in the fields, feeding hogs, or cutting hair, there were not more than one or two times he did not have on a white shirt and suspenders. He always wore suspenders. We grew up not having much of anything. We were too broke to know that we were broke, but we never went hungry. He was a great provider and knew how to make things work out. Daddy would always say, 'Keep a dollar in your pocket." To this day, I remember that.

We lived about one mile from school, which we were made to attend every day, unlike some of our older siblings who had to skip school at times in order to go pick cotton. We also picked pecans and dewberries with my father, which we sold on the highway roadside. Every time we made any money, we had to give him some of it, which was fair.

Mama Newsome was always a self-employed man. The only time I remember him working for someone had lasted, I think, for 3 or 4 weeks. My understanding is that he quit because he didn't like someone telling him what to do.

Mama was a farmer by trade, raising chickens, hogs, and pigs. He also planted cotton and corn. I think he also pretty much built one of the homes we lived in. I remember that we had to feed the animals every day. He also cut hair for a living. He cut most of the guys' hair in our small town. He had a barber shop downtown, and he would sometimes cut hair at home if necessary. The shop had one barber chair, not like the barber chairs you see in this day and age.

He also later got a pool table in the shop. He liked it when I would come around, because at times I would have a few other guys around with me, and we would play pool. It cost 25 cents per game to play, so that was another way for him to bring in some change. I am self-employed, as are most of my siblings, so I guess it runs in our genes to be financially independent.

I left home in 1972 to go into the service. I remember him telling me to be careful out yonder. When I left the service, I went straight home. They were so glad to see me back and were sad when I left again in just a couple of weeks to move to Kansas City.

When we would come home from Kansas City to visit, the first thing he would ask was, 'You didn't drive like a bat out of Hell, did you?' Then I would say, I might've driven 75-80 mph. He would say, 'Boy, you know that was too fast!' My father was a slow driver, but Mother was a fast driver.

One of Daddy's favorite cartoons was The Flintstones. He would sit back in his white undershirt, relaxing in his rocking chair and laughing at the show. While relaxing in his chair, sometimes he would call my mother, and say, 'Ina, bring me some of that cream!' My wife gets on to me to this day because she thinks I wait for her or my granddaughter who lives with us to ask for something out of the kitchen. I guess I got that from him.

When Daddy liked something, or agreed with something, he would say, 'That will get it!' Any time he was supposed to do something later, he would say, 'If nothing happens!' Now, my father was a man who did not like to travel. He was content right where he was. If he came to visit us in Kansas City for an engagement, and the engagement was over at four, he was ready then to head back home. He was a respectful man, with a unique character, who was loved by many.

Chapter 10
Delores F. Newsome-French

I was the tenth of eleven children born to John Douglas (J. D.) Newsome and Ina Turknett. I called my father "Daddy" and my mother "Madear." Daddy was much younger of course when my older siblings were growing up, so as you can imagine their memories of him might be quite different from mine. I finished high school and left home two months before my 17th birthday.

My paternal grandparents, Lottie Mays (Mama Lottie) and Philip Newsome, Jr. (Daddy Bud) had four sons (Artie Dell, Willie B., John Douglas & James Columbus); the youngest two were my daddy (John) and his twin brother, (James), whom we called Uncle J. C. People in my hometown, Chappell Hill, Texas, called Uncle J. C. "Papa" Newsome and they called my daddy "Mama" Newsome. How their nicknames originated, I'm not certain. His nieces, nephews and some grandchildren would refer to him as Daddy J. D. Most of his grandchildren would refer to him as Daddy, just as his own children did.

We lived on a small farm a few miles from downtown Chappell Hill that Mama Lottie, my very independent grandmother, worked very hard to purchase. Daddy's brothers moved to Houston, but he married my mother and they continued to live in Chappell Hill and raised their eleven children on the family farm. Mama Lottie's house was just up the hill from our house, about a one-minute walk away.

One of the most vivid things I remember as a child about Daddy was his fear of storms or threatening weather. Our house was not considered well-made or foundationally strong, but my grandmother had a much nicer house. After all, as mentioned earlier, she worked hard to acquire what she had after she and my grandfather were divorced. Because Mama Lottie's house was considered "better built," whenever the dark clouds began to head our way, Daddy would make the entire family leave our home and walk to Mama Lottie's house to ride the storm out. Whenever there was thunder, lightning or heavy rain, Daddy required us to sit still and be quiet. He and other adults referred to such weather as ***God at work***.

Anyone would tell you Daddy was not a perfect man, husband, or father, and he showed very few, if any, endearing emotions or outward signs of affection. Somehow though, my general sense and memory of Daddy was that he loved us, and he did his best to provide for his family.

I've heard stories from older siblings and family members about how Daddy struggled with alcohol when they were growing up, but they also talked about how he at some point made the decision to stop drinking and was able to quit cold turkey. To me, the story of how he was able to stop told me more about Daddy's strong will and determination to do right by his family than anything else. I'm told that he stopped drinking on July 10th, 1955, before I was born, and never touched a drink again. I think this news about Daddy, along with the fact that Madear never touched alcohol, had a strong influence on mine and my siblings' attitude toward alcohol throughout our adult years.

One of my memories of Daddy was that his tone of voice was one that commonly sounded as if he was fussing or mad about something. I don't recall having many one-on-one conversations with Daddy when I was growing up. I don't recall going anywhere with Daddy, just the two of us, and if there had been such a thing as a father/daughter dance, I guarantee you, he would not have taken me. There was no such thing as a father/daughter relationship to speak of; that kind of relationship was not a thing back in those days. Madear used to play around and pretend to kiss him, and he would act like he didn't like it and would tell her to get off of him. As we got older, my siblings and I would tell Daddy "I love you" and ask him to tell us he loves us. He was never comfortable with saying that but would always reply with, "I love all y'all." In spite of his lack of positive emotions or outward displays of affection, I've always regarded him as a good father and a decent man. Most of the verbal communication happened between me and Madear, whom I was more comfortable with, and she would communicate to Daddy what he needed to know.

Daddy was only about 5′ 6″ tall, but he was never intimidated by his height. Though most of my brothers grew to be taller than Daddy, they clearly knew disrespecting him was not an option, and they never verbally questioned his authority.

Daddy was a farmer and required my brothers to work hard and pick cotton to earn money for the family. Not only was he a farmer, but he was also a barber, and had a small shop in downtown Chappell Hill. On Saturdays, he would go there to cut haircuts and maybe one or two other days of the week, by appointment only. He also worked "remotely" as people would also come to our house for their haircuts. I never knew until recent years just how meticulous Daddy was about organization and recordkeeping. I was given one of his ledgers/journals where he tracked all of his customers as a barber, their appointment times, the fees he charged, etc. I realize that my gift of organization and recordkeeping must have come from him. People always tease me about Excel and using spreadsheets. I truly believe that if that technology had been around during Daddy's time, he would have been a spreadsheet geek.

We never had much money growing up. As I look back on my life then, we were actually poor but were never made to feel like we were poor or less than. I can remember hearing Daddy say, "Y'all must think money grows on trees." The interesting thing about it is, so I'm told, that Daddy was never ever completely broke; he always believed in "putting back" and saving a little of what he did have, though everyone else didn't necessarily know about it.

Daddy was a member of Ebenezer Missionary Baptist Church and Madear was a member of St. John AME Church. Attending separate churches never seemed to be an issue for them. Though Daddy didn't attend church every Sunday, he was a praying man. Seeing and occasionally hearing my father pray made me feel he took his relationship with Christ seriously.

Daddy also knew scripture. Later in his years, I had the awesome blessing of hearing him recite Psalm 27 in its entirety from memory. I had no idea!!! Experiencing this gave me a whole new level of admiration and respect for my daddy.

Daddy and Madear were committed to their children developing their own relationship with Christ. Neither were big on us accepting Christ by just going down the aisle and shaking the preacher's hand ("joining" church). He and my mother were in agreement that each child needed to go to the mourner's bench to "get religion." During this period of focused prayer, seeking God, and confessing sins, even Daddy allowed a temporary break from the everyday chores.

Though he himself would not have been considered super spiritual, he was conscious about how his children ought to live. If he heard us playing secular music on the radio, he would tell us, 'Y'all going to hell listening to those blues." Though Daddy discontinued drinking alcohol at the age of 43, Uncle J. C. continued until his death. Unlike Uncle J. C., who gambled (throwing dice) in his later years, Daddy no longer indulged in gambling and tried to discourage his children from engaging in it. He stopped drinking, smoking, and gambling but never stopped using the spicy language.

One unique thing about Daddy and his twin brother was that they always wore white shirts - every day. Daddy could be feeding the hogs or chickens, and he'd be wearing a white shirt. He was not into style. In fact, I remember hearing him say something like "folks going to Hell trying to keep up with the style." Sometimes he'd ask me to wash his shirts and he or Madear would pretend there might be something in the pocket for me, as if I'd be paid for the task. I don't recall, but I must have received a nickel or quarter a couple of times for removing the ring around the collar of his white shirts.

Daddy was pretty strict with me as his baby girl. During high school, there were boys who I liked and who liked me, but the idea of dating or having an official boyfriend was not readily welcomed. There was one boy I liked, and I was told he was my cousin. I remember visiting one of my friends, Alecia Davis, who had several brothers. I was not interested in them, nor were they interested in me, but I remember Daddy making me come home when he felt I was visiting her too long. I got the sense he felt it just wasn't a good idea for me to be around boys. The boys I did like, I got the chance to see during school hours only. Looking back on it now, I think my relationship with the opposite sex was not as healthy as it could have been. I'm not blaming it on Daddy, but I don't believe either parent was helpful in teaching me how to have healthy dating relationships. Several years after high school and my move to Kansas City, I got pregnant with Jayneice. When Daddy found out I was pregnant, I don't recall if he said it to me directly, but he was concerned that once I started having babies, that I would keep having them. Eventually, after meeting my husband Jeff, I took him home to meet Daddy. One of the things Jeff remembers about Daddy was him saying "A man isn't a real man if he doesn't carry a handkerchief." Once he discovered that Jeff used and carried a handkerchief, that sealed the deal and Jeff was a keeper.

In 1969, my older siblings had a new house built for my parents and the younger children who were still living at home. The really cool thing about this house was that it had indoor plumbing!!! In spite of this modern convenience, for a while, Daddy continued to use the outdoor toilet for #2 because he just couldn't imagine the idea of anyone doing that inside the house. He used more graphic language to describe the situation.

Daddy was a no-nonsense kind of guy and most of the time he seemed quite serious. I don't recall him smiling or laughing much, but I do remember a few rare times that he told jokes or got tickled about something he saw on television. We were amused when he played around and spoke a little Polish or Pig Latin. Madear was always the more jovial person and she and the granddaughters often found things to laugh about and "made a lot of noise." Jayneice (my daughter) recalls him often saying "y'all sho' can grin." He wasn't very outgoing and didn't have many friends or much of a social life that I was aware of, but he and Madear enjoyed playing dominoes and being competitive.

The memories I have of Daddy often make me smile. I enjoy hearing my older siblings talk about their memories of Daddy and all the things he used to say. When I went home to Chappell Hill, Texas to visit my parents, upon pulling up in the driveway, it was not uncommon to see Daddy sitting in his chair looking out the window. That was his favorite spot in his later years. During my last trip home to see Daddy, in November of 1995, he was not sitting in that chair, because he was sick in the hospital. My oldest brother, Robert, and I rushed home to be by his side about five hours before he passed. We joined Madear, my sisters and my nieces there and were all around his bedside as he breathed his last breath. We told him we loved him. I can only imagine Daddy saying in response "I LOVE ALL Y'ALL."

Chapter 11
Oscar W. Newsome

One of the greatest mysteries I had growing up was why my father was called "Mama' or "Mama Newsome."

I mean, my father's given name was "John Douglas" Newsome, yet everyone in the town called him "Mama." My mother and my brothers and sisters never called him that. But, all my life, this was the only name I ever heard. To me he was "Daddy," not "Mama."

I was the baby of the family - a family of 11 children. I stayed at home until I was 20 years old, longer than any of my brothers and sisters. I was always called "My Baby" by my mother...but not by my daddy. My daddy was a straight-laced, no-nonsense fellow. He had his way of doing things. He was never influenced by anyone else in the world. For Daddy, he was the law; he had the last word. He didn't really have any friends. He had business relationships with other people but no real friends.

Most of my brothers and sisters grew up picking cotton and doing other field work. Being the youngest, I only picked a little cotton on our small farm.

I did not escape from many of the other farm chores. My daddy made sure that I knew how to do many other things. He taught me how to care for and feed the pigs and the chickens, and to care for our two dogs.

My dad and I did a few things together, yet, we did not have much of a relationship. Dad and I would go out and pick pecans, take them to the stores, and sell them. My dad let me help him castrate the pigs and get them ready for the auction. My dad bought me a .410-shotgun and he and I went hunting for rabbits and quail. Dad did not have a gun, but he trained the dogs to chase after the rabbits and to pick up the quails I shot. He never wanted the dogs to come inside the house.

Dad was never an affectionate person. I never saw him hug or kiss my mother. Whenever my mother would playfully try to hug and kiss him, he would push her away. Dad never hugged his children or told us he loved us. If we said, "Dad, do you love me?" His response would always be, "I love all of y'all!" He would leave it at that, but we were never phased by his response. He just had his own way of expressing himself in that manner: he cared for his family, he provided for his family, and for us, that was enough for me. I hugged him when I left for the Army.

He seemed to always be busy. He did some work on our small farm. He was a barber and had a small barber shop in town. Sometimes people would come to the house for a haircut; sometimes he would go to the people's houses to cut their hair, but it did not matter to him just as long as he could get the job done.

Daddy never really gave us instructions about life and living. He tried, instead to live and practice his message: he never said, this is how you should do this or that, he just did things and expected us to learn from him doing. He corrected me with his words. I never got a spanking from my dad nor my mother.

I joined the Army at the age of 20, the same year that I finished high school. My dad and mother took me to the bus station. I do not remember ever having any contact with Dad during the 6 years I was in the Army.

My dad was a good man and took care of business. He did not give me any special treatment. This was just his character. My dad was a holy man in his own way. He read his Bible, prayed for his family, and went to church pretty much every Sunday.

"The Man Called Mama" is my daddy!

Chapter 12
Last Sibling, Early Bee Kemp

Hello, my name is Early Bee Kemp. I was born on August 18th, 1969, in Brenham, Texas. My daddy was J. D. Newsome, also known as "Mama" Newsome. My daddy had a barber shop just off the main street in downtown Chappell Hill, Texas. Chappell Hill is a small town where almost everyone knows one another, and everyone seems to know everyone else's business.

Before I was born, my daddy was married and had 11 children. I was his 12th and last child. I am the baby boy. My dad was not married to my mother, but he treated me with love and respect. I was not with him always, and he never lived with us. He used to come to our house to visit. He took me places around the town in his pickup truck and took me shopping on several occasions in Brenham, about 10 miles from Chappell Hill. He was a good guy. He never told me he loved me, but he showed his love for me by doing what I mentioned. He talked to me and gave me good advice. He would get in my butt when I was slow about doing things, he told me to do. He always told me to go to school and avoid trouble. A lot of people told me to stay out of trouble. I only sometimes listened because I had my mind and wanted to experience some things and do them my way. I remember him saying: *"A hard head makes a soft ass!"* Now I wish I had listened to him more because I got into trouble a few times. I should have remembered his warning when he said: *"Son, don't write a check that your ass can't cash!"* Looking at the wise counsel and advice he gave me, I find myself wishing he was still here. Even though he is not here physically, I can still hear his voice ringing in my ears at times. Now that I think about it, when I laugh, I sound just like him; when I listen to myself talking, I talk like him. Many of my ways are just like my daddy's ways.

Daddy also showed me how to work. I spent time with him cutting grass, cutting wood, and hauling wood. He used the wood for the wood-burning stove in his one-room barber shop. When I was a little older, I visited his barber shop almost daily. When some men around town came by his shop, he made them cut the wood and put it in the stove. Some of the men went into the shop to seek his advice. Most of the time, they came by the shop to have a place to drink their Thunderbird wine. I never saw him take a drink because he had stopped drinking many years before. Sometimes the men would gamble, but I never saw him gamble. There was one thing he did very well, and that was cussing. He would cuss about anything, and he would cuss to anybody.

Daddy did not tell me much about his other eleven children. He told me that most of his children lived in Kansas City and were in real estate. He always talked about Robert, his oldest child. He said Robert had moved to Kansas City in his teenage years and had started a real estate company. I can remember the very first time I met Robert. My dad brought him by my mom's house to meet me. Robert asked me if I knew who he was. I responded, *"Kind of. Sort of."* Then Robert said, *"I am your oldest brother, and glad to meet you!"* I told him that I was glad to meet him too. Robert also came to the barber shop a time or two when he was in town. He *always "slipped a few nickels in my pocket whenever I saw him."* Daddy always seemed happy when Robert was around.

I also met my daddy's other children. Joyce was the only child who lived in Chappell Hill. Joyce and

I, *we kicked it!* She is cool! One day she saw me walking down the street and told me I better take my butt to school. She gave me summer sausage and cheese when I was in the halfway house in Bryan, Texas. She reminds me of my daddy a lot because her feisty attitude is similar to my daddy's.

One of the sweetest moments of my life happened when I was younger, and I met my daddy's wife at the barber shop. She asked me, *"Do you want to be my little boy?"* I said, "Yes." I felt good and started laughing. I was thrilled when she bought me some ice cream and cookies. I don't think I ever went out to her house.

Daddy was kind of a blunt guy, and, in many ways, I am just like him. He always said what he wanted to say...and so do I. People tell me that I am a *"smarty."* I tell them I got it from my daddy. I tell them how I feel and, if they like it or don't like it, it does not matter to me, *"they can just kick rocks!"* I told Joyce I often laugh and talk like my daddy. I told her that being the baby guy, sometimes it seems like I laugh, talk, and have many ways like Daddy more than the rest of his children do. It makes me feel good! But I don't feel I am more like my daddy than the rest of his children because we all have his blood.

My dad was particular about the way he looked. I never saw him in a short-sleeved shirt. He only wore white shirts. With a toothpick hanging from his mouth, he would spit through his teeth. Even if a speck of spit got on his shirt, he would immediately get up, go home, and change his shirt. Sometimes he would take a newspaper, leave the barber shop, go uptown, spread the paper on the concrete porch, and sit down on it to remain clean.

Daddy talked about spiritual things with me a few times. He went to church, but I never went with him. He never invited me to go with him. But he used to tell me, *"Boy, you better get your mind right and start taking your butt to church!"* He never prayed with me, but he always told me he prayed for me. Telling me he prayed for me made me feel he cared. I loved the guy, but I don't think I ever told him I did. I catch myself thinking about him all the time. If I could say one thing to him right now, I would tell him I love him. Even though he and I did not have that *"I love you"* thing going on, I wanted all his children to know I loved the man.

Another thing I gave some thought to over the years about my daddy, that I dared not ask him, was why he got involved with another woman when he already had a wonderful wife and eleven children. I dared not ask him because I was not in his business like that. I had no good answers except, *"I don't know...it happens...we be out there...I guess we call it 'hot'!"* "I say *"we."* What my Daddy did is just *"life,"* and life happens to all of us in one form or another. Sadly, I don't know what I learned from my daddy's behavior.

There are a couple more things I want to share about my daddy. These things are not connected, but I want to share them anyway. It must have been challenging to raise 11 children and then give birth to me. Even still, he did not neglect me. He did provide help for my mother when he could. I know he loved his 11 children and all their children. I respected him for that.

When I was getting ready to marry, he called me and said he wanted to see me. I could not get to him, but I think he would've said, *"Son, don't do that!"* I believe that he did not want me to get married and then do the same thing he did. But I got married. Anyway, my marriage lasted for *"15 minutes."*

I was not with him when he took sick, nor did I visit him in the hospital. I never wanted to bother him. I regret that I did not always follow his advice. I regret being in jail instead of spending more time with him. Lastly, I regret not being with him when he took his last breath. Even until this day, I think about him and laugh. I think about him and cry. I think about some of his funny sayings, like:

- "Boy, I need money more than a hog needs slop!"

- "He was as scared as a possum with an ax handle 'round his neck!"
- "Bull corn!"
- "It's as cold as a well digger's ass in Montana!"
- "Well, hell, boy!"

My Daddy wore Stacy Adams shoes. He told me, *"If you ever buy a pair of Stacy's, make sure you got the ones with the Adams on it. Otherwise, you ain't got shit!"*

I remember the time he cooked a swamp rabbit and made brown gravy. I am happy to have a closer relationship with many of my siblings.
A few years ago, I was at my sister Joyce's house in Chappell Hill after my daddy died. I felt some of my siblings did not want to meet with me. But, before the day was gone, some told me I was sounding and acting just like my daddy. That was such a compliment to me and made me feel really good. I left that day feeling that I had been accepted. I could imagine Daddy smiling down from heaven to see how we were carrying on.

Lastly, I discovered that all my brothers and sisters were writing a book called "A Man Called Mama."

Each one was writing about what they remembered about Daddy and how he impacted and influenced their lives. When one of my siblings called and told me what they were doing, and invited me to write my version, I almost had tears because it made me feel like I was a genuine part of the family.

Chapter 13
Robert L. Newsome, Jr.
Oldest Grandson

The man called Mama was my granddaddy. I had the great fortune to spend about six months with him in the summer of 1988. I was having some issues in my life and my daddy thought it would be helpful for me to have a change of scenery by spending some time in the country with my grandfather on his farm.

I never knew why my grandfather was called Mama, and I never asked him. I do know that everyone in the small town of Chappell Hill, Texas referred to him as Mama, yet I also know that such a name is unusual for a man. I had to make many adjustments being there on the farm and in this small town. It was not my choice to be there. My daddy felt I could learn to be a better person if I spent time under the stricter leadership of my grandfather. Until that time, I had only visited my granddaddy occasionally.

My grandfather did not mind me being there and he actually welcomed me. True to form, he "laid down the law" and instructed me to do things I had never done before: feeding the pigs, pulling corn, and hauling hay. It did not take him long to find out that I was a city boy! The pigs were nasty and pulling corn and hauling hay was too hot. He never asked why I had decided to come to stay with him, and frankly, I don't think he really cared, because once I was there, he decided to put me to work helping him by doing what he would have had to do. I think he and my father had already discussed putting me to work doing these unpleasant chores. Being there with him made me appreciate the life my father had to endure. He was good to me and good for me. He was not playful, but he was not unkind.

My grandfather was quite a character. He was a no-nonsense person who couldn't care less about what other people thought about him or anything else. He said what was on his mind and was not bothered by what your thoughts were. I don't think I ever saw him laugh or smile. He was the sternest person I ever knew. Deep down within, I think he had a softer side, but I felt that he had to develop a certain sternness to survive. Nobody messed with him. He displayed some of his favorite curse words at the drop of a hat. That was his aggressive side. I never saw him angry or mistreating anyone. He always had a gun, but he never displayed it. I think it made him feel safe, but I never inquired of him as to why he was "packing". The only thing I ever saw him do with a gun was in preparation of food for the family when he, with one shot to the head, brought the hog down and hung the animal on the side of the house to allow the blood to drip out. This was a customary way to kill the hog but was certainly nothing I was prepared to do.

I visited his barber shop on several occasions and observed how he interacted with other people. He was always in control of the conversation whether he initiated it or not. He would express his opinion about the veracity of the assertions of another and would let a person know if he thought they were lying or not. He never said, "Yes, you are telling the truth!" He always cursed about things that others would say but I never heard him curse another person.

He always gave me sound advice. He encouraged me to take care of my own business and leave others alone. He advised me not to drink and drive. He advised me to take care of my family.

My grandfather was very proud of his children. He was especially proud of my father whom he talked about very often.

To others, he was a man called Mama, but to me he was my grandfather.

Bio:
Robert L Newsome, Jr.
The oldest grandchild of Mama Newsome
Graduated Southeast High School Kansas City, Missouri
Military Service: Short stint in the United States Army
Work History: Worked many years in the mental health industry.

Chapter 14
Monica R. Lewis-Edmond
Oldest Granddaughter

When I first heard about the book "A Man Called Mama", I thought it was going to be written by the children of J. D. Newsome. After finding out the children as well as grandchildren would have the opportunity to contribute, I began to have an array of emotions; honor, gratitude, fear, and anxiety. Honor, because I am proud to be the oldest granddaughter of this "Man Called Mama". Gratitude, because I am grateful to be a part of a well-respected Newsome Legacy. The fear and anxiety partly come from not knowing what I should say, and not wanting to say something wrong.

When I hear the phrase "A Man Called Mama", I think of a man small in stature who was also a gentle giant in my eyes. He loved his family. Though we may have not heard the words "I love you", we just knew and understood it was so.

As a child I remembered going to Daddy and Madea's for the summer and spending the entire day outside playing. One summer that really sticks out in my mind was when my cousins Bridgette and Charlotte (and I can't remember who else) were outside playing in the dirt, and he made us plant potatoes. We had to dig the holes and put water in them to make it muddy.

We were trying to be cute and not get so dirty, and Daddy came over, bent down, and said "S--- you gotta push the potatoes down in there" and proceeded to take one of our hands and push it in the muddy mess. Man, we were mad at him! Until this very day we get a laugh about that.

Celebrating Christmas was my absolute all-time favorite. We could expect a real Christmas tree (cut down by him), plenty of fruit, nuts, and Christmas candy; you know the ones shaped like little ribbons. There weren't many gifts from Madea and Daddy because there were so many of us, but you were sure to get a pair of socks and some undies. We would sit around in the living room where there was a wood-burning stove and play and talk until we were told to go to bed so Santa could make his arrival.

Another time I remember is when we had to carry well water for bath time. Yep, we carried water from my great grandmother's (Mama Lottie) back to the house. Then we had to boil it in pots on the stove and pour it into a round metal tub that sat in the middle of the living room to take our baths! Thank God for change & modernization!

As an adult, I often wonder why we say and do some of the things we do. Sometimes it's as simple as picking it up from those who came before us. For instance, ironing on a Sunday was a definite no-no, or during a storm sitting quietly with the TV off. I specifically remember in the summer of 1982 during hurricane Alicia how we had to tape all the windows. We had to sit quietly in the hallway and try to keep from giggling.

My grandfather owned his own barber shop. He was the owner, worker & bookkeeper all rolled into one. I have possession of his business ledger and on the outside, it is titled "JDN 1964, Wednesday June 17th. Inside the dates span over four or five years -from April of 1960 to 1964. It details the names of his customers and the amounts they paid for their haircuts. I guess this is where I picked up on some of my organizational skills. I even found a record of my then future father-in-law who coincidentally was named JD. The line entry reads "JD Edmond boy 4/4/1962, $.75". That was my husband Hippie who was about 1 1/2 years old at the time. The ledger also included things like when his mother had her will made out for her sons--Monday, May 13, 1963, at George R. Moorman Attorney at Law; he and my grandmother were present. On that same day he bought a ballpoint pen for $.98. He entered weather days of continuous rain, who he gave money to for goods and services, who borrowed money, or who he gave credit to for haircuts; My mother's address at 2014 Cleburne St., scriptures, and texts and notes from sermons were also noted. The assassination of President JFK was noted 11/22/1963 @ 1:15 p.m., Friday. Reverend

MLK was killed on Thursday 4/4/1968, and this too was recorded in his ledger.

So many things about this "Man Called Mama' bring a smile to my face as well as a sadness to my heart; when I think of him sitting near the living room window in his old recliner chair with a spit bucket (an old Folgers coffee can) used for his snuff, eating out of the same tin plate, sitting on the front porch in his old wooden chair, standing in the doorway with one arm propped wearing a pair of slacks, wearing a white tank t-shirt with a pair of suspenders or dressed to the 9's with his Sunday-go-to-meeting attire.

While I have no regrets, I do wish I could have heard more stories about the "old days" when he was a boy picking cotton and when my mom, and her siblings were children.

Finally, I tip my hat, take a bow and curtsey to say thank you to this 'Man Called Mama' for his intentional and unintentional lessons about life, hard work (like planting those potatoes), and struggle (carrying all those buckets of water). It really makes me appreciate being able to go to the grocery store to buy potatoes or turn on the faucet to run my bath water.

Chapter 15
Autiquawa Lewis-Cousin
Granddaughter

Sitting on the porch . . .

Sitting in his chair in the living room . . .

Working in his barber shop . . .

These were things you would typically see when it came to John Douglas Newsome., Daddy, Mama.

Sitting out on the porch . . . in that wooden folding chair looking out at God's wonders, what was he thinking about? I wish I would have asked him that question. I believe my grandfather was a great thinker.

He had to have been with the life he lived. I can see him now, his snuff can on the ground, and him periodically lifting it to spit. As a kid, I had strange feelings about this, but I didn't dare say a word! When we had family reunions, he would watch us grandkids playing.

Sometimes he'd have a smile on his face, and sometimes with that rough, fussing tone he'd tell one of us to, "Get away from there!" Wow! As a kid, I thought he was mean, and I tried everything I could not to be the object of his harshness. As an adult, I now know this was his way of showing love and being protective.

Sitting in his chair in the living room . . . by the window, you could often see him either looking out, wanting Ina to do something, or watching TV. I know he loved my grandmother. I never heard him say it, but it was just something you couldn't help but know.

Instead, what I'd hear was, "Ina, why don't you . . .?" That tone was everything. My grandmother was a meek and gentle presence, and my grandfather was just the opposite. It seems like a negative thing, but it really wasn't. That was Daddy. You just understood. Even with that, one of his favorite shows was Charlie Brown. I thought that was the cutest thing! A smile could be brought to my rough grandfather's face by merely watching a cartoon! Again, what was he thinking about? What brought that smile?

Working at the barbershop . . . I thought it was so great that my grandfather owned a business. He was a man of many talents, one of which was being a barber. In that small, dark, shanty building, he kept meticulous records of his work, customers, and payments. Saturdays were the days we visited our grandparents. Part of those visits sometimes included a stop at Daddy's barbershop. Many people went to him for their haircuts. Often that rough tone came out when he worked, but that never stopped his customers from returning because they not only knew that he knew what he was doing but also, they knew that was just "Mama" Newsome. What did he think about that business and those people?

John Douglas (Mama) Newsome was strong, tough, and often a man of few words, but he was my grandfather.
A provider.
A strong presence.
A thinker.

Chapter 16
Travis A. Newsome (Lexy)
Grandson

One would presume that a man named Mama is an interesting character, to say the least, and I can confirm that to be accurate. Mama Newsome, my father's father, was truly one of a kind. He was tough yet humorous, no-nonsense and yet simple, a humble man who feared God yet knew how to cause others to fear him. This description of my grandfather might seem contradictory to some, but upon careful consideration of my personal accounts with him that I'm about to share, it will become clear as to why I chose these words with which to honor his legacy. While I don't recall my specific age when these events occurred, as I was young at the time, the memory of them remains vivid in my mind.

"Sit Down Boy"

By trade, Daddy J.D. was a barber who worked out of his own shop in downtown Chappell Hill, Texas. I'm not sure how many times my parents had my grandfather cut my hair. My mother didn't seem too fond of the idea and to be honest neither did I. Quite frankly, I was scared to death to sit in that barber's chair. On one end, some might say that this was natural. After all, the sound of an old-school electric shaver near your head when you're young can be startling. Still, it was the way that Daddy J.D. seemed to go about cutting my hair. Now, when I get my hair cut, my barber is respectful, we have good conversation, and for the most part, it's a pleasant experience. This was not quite the case with Daddy J.D. though. I remember one time sitting in his chair, feeling one hand pressed against the top of my head, at times to hold me still so that he could do his work, while at other times aggressively turning my head to cut a different section. I didn't have the sense of being in a comfortable space, nor was my grandfather laughing or sharing wisdom with me about life as in some special moment of bonding. No, in that moment, all I felt was that this old man with a frown on his face was violently twisting my head every which way with clippers at a space that was uncomfortably close to my face. All the while, with a stern, gruff tone saying, "Sit still, boy! Sit still!" The good news is that I survived that haircut, though not a hair on my head did.

"You Won't Eat All That"

One time while in Chappell Hill, my father, Daddy J.D., and I went and had breakfast at the local diner off of the main highway. Growing up, I ate a lot, and it showed. Let's just say that I don't think that anyone ever had a concern as to whether I was getting enough to eat. On this particular occasion, I ordered pancakes. When our breakfast arrived, Daddy J.D. leaned in toward the table and slightly towards me with an expression that was the combination of a scowl and a smirk saying, "You're not going to eat all of those pancakes boy." Looking back on it, it was probably his own unique way of saying, "Boy! You know you're already too big and don't need to eat all of those pancakes." Yet still, because of the way that he said it, I took it as a challenge. I wanted to prove him wrong, so I foolishly scarfed down the entire plate of pancakes making myself sick but acting like I was fine. When I finished, he glanced at me with that same scowl and smirk as if he could see right through me and knew that deep down, I had no business eating all of those pancakes. Seeming to still want to get under my skin, he said to me, when you get home say this to your sister. He then proceeded to speak something in Polish and began to laugh. At this point, someone might be wondering about why a black man in rural Texas would be able to speak Polish. This is due to the fact that Chappell Hill was settled by Polish immigrants, but I digress. To this day, I have absolutely no idea what the translation of what he said was, but I know it wasn't good because, immediately afterward, my father responded by rolling his eyes and saying to me, "No, don't say that." My father never told me why I should not speak those Polish words to my sister Maria-Alicia. I am certain he did not know what they meant, but because of my grandfather's proclivity for using four letter words, we can only assume it must have been a connection.

"Don't Call Me Grandpa"

Of all the memories I have of my grandfather, the one that stands out the most happened at his house. I had been playing outside and had come into the living room. Towards the end of his life, he had become accustomed to sitting in a particular chair in the corner of the room.

When I saw him, I said, "Hi Grandpa!" I meant this as a kind gesture but would soon learn that I had made a major mistake. He had me sit on the floor and began to lecture me about why I was never to call him "grandpa." By his reaction, one would've thought that I had called him a four-letter word. Honestly, I don't remember a single word of what he said, other than the message of not to call him Grandpa. So then, ever since, I made sure to call him Daddy J.D.

Conclusion

The Wife
Ina Newsome

{This posthumously written story is about Ina Newsome, and her relationship with boyfriend and husband J.D. "Mama" Newsome. Ina (Mudear) died on July 4th,1997. Travis wrote this story by secretly interviewing his siblings regarding conversation they had with Mudear over the years}

I know y'all didn't think I was going to sit idly by as you wrote about J. D., did you? Yes, he was Daddy to y'all, even the older grandchildren called him Daddy while the younger ones called him Daddy J. D. Nieces and nephews called him Uncle J. D. Everyone else called him Mama Newsome, but he was J. D. (John Douglas) to me. While everyone else is talking about Daddy, Daddy J. D., Uncle J.D., and Mama Newsome, please allow me to tell you a few things about J. D., my husband, for over 58 and a half years.

I don't recall the exact date I met J. D. but I do know it was in the summer of 1935 when he showed up at the grocery store where I was with my sister S. J. I had just turned 19 a few days earlier. He wanted to walk us home but we knew that would not be a good idea. Papa Turknett (my father) was not having any of that even though I was grown at 19. I thought he was sorta cute with good hair but he was pretty short, and that made me not interested. A week later, I ran into him again at the same store around the same time. He confessed that he had returned to the store for the past six days in a row at the same time praying he would see me there. I thought to myself, *what is that all about? He really must be interested in me but he is much older.* We sat behind the store on a bench and talked for a few minutes before it was time for me to go home. J. D. was very intriguing to me - probably because I had never had a serious boyfriend before. I did not see him again for quite some time. When I did, he asked me if he could come by my home and I said yes. After that, we would see each other more frequently. I guess we were (what is called in this day and age), "dating." This was in early 1936. We continued to date and things got pretty serious. We ended up getting married on April 10th, 1937. Our first child. Robert Lee, was born 5 weeks later on May 18th, 1937. I was in love and continued to love J. D. beyond his death in 1995.

Why was I so in love with this man? Afterall, he had a drinking problem that got progressively worse over the first 17 years of our marriage. He was a Christian who did not attend church regularly. All I could do was pray, and that I did. J. D. was the epitome of a functioning alcoholic. He was never, I mean never, abusive toward me or the kids, even when he had had too much to drink. He was a great provider. I knew I could always depend upon him. He stopped drinking in 1954 and never took another drink. Thank you, God, for prayers answered.

Our second child, Johnnie Mae was born more than three years after Robert. We did not talk about having a second child. We did not even discuss or plan to have our first child. After Johnnie Mae, you see there were 9 more children. We never discussed how many children we would have. They just kept coming, and coming, strong and healthy. I am so thankful for all of them. After our 11th child, Oscar, I was finished. J. D. was not. He stepped outside of the marriage and had another child, Early Kemp. J. D. asked for forgiveness for his transgression and my Christianity allowed me to say, "Yes, I forgive you." I must admit, it was not easy, "BUT GOD!"

J. D. was a good man loved by me and all the kids. The kids always respected him. Not once did I hear one of the kids talk back to J. D.

This book was the kids' idea so I am not trying to steal their thunder.

Let me be concise and very clear. I believe the readers have been shown a very clear picture here about how families should strive to live and love. My prayer is that families find evidence here of the power of forgiveness, and of the protection and strength that unity provides. Families should do whatever is necessary to maintain a good family structure. Our family was the wealthiest family in Chappell Hill. No amount of money could purchase the strong bond and love we had which was the source of that wealth.

I am very proud of how we raised our eleven children. The fact that no one has been arrested or charged with a crime and no one has ever spent a night in jail speaks volumes. That is not bad for our 8 black boys whose years of living on this earth have exceeded 596 years at the publication of this book. It speaks volumes as it relates to how we tried to live a Christian-centered life.

To my children:
I would like to express my sincere thanks for each of you for the love and respect you all displayed towards us. Thank you for this book.

Your Mom,
I love all y'all, too!

Mudear (Ina)

Travis Newsome

Biography

Like his siblings, Travis' early life was in Chappell Hill, Texas. He graduated from Brenham High School in 1969 after being one of nine black students to fully integrate the high school 4 years earlier. He received a full athletic scholarship to the University of Oklahoma where he excelled in track. Travis graduated from Oklahoma with a finance degree in the spring of 1973. Upon graduation, he took with him two school records (Quarter Mile and Mile Relay). Travis was selected as a part of an all-Christian team to tour 8 countries in West and East Africa, and Israel in 1972 to do missionary work (passing up an opportunity to qualify for the 1972 USA Olympic team for which he had qualified to compete).

Travis moved to Kansas City, MO, to assist with the family real estate business after graduation from Oklahoma. He became president of the company in 1974 as promised by his brother Robert during Christmas break when he was in the 8th grade. He remained president for the next 37 years. Travis was involved in many organizations and served on many boards including having served for 29 years on the billion-dollar Blue Cross Blue Shield Board of Kansas City, MO, where for a time he was Vice-Chairman of the Board.

Travis met Maryalice Davis on July 28th, 1974,

and they got married on July 26th, 1975. Three years later on July 4th, 1978, their first child Maria-Alicia Serrano. Their second Child Travis Alexis was born April 18th, 1981. They currently have 4 four granddaughters.

This is Travis' 3rd book. His first book, "Play Dominoes Like A Champion" (self-published, Amazon) was released on his birthday, November 28th, 2021. His second book, "Dominoes Game Night: 65 Classic Games To Entertain and Excite," is scheduled to be released on June 27th, 2023 (Black Dog and Leventhal Publishers).

Travis is a three-time world champion domino player. He was the first African American to win the World Domino Championship Tournament in Alabama, in 1988. Travis continues to compete in domino tournaments, and plays dominoes online every day. He also teaches his online domino class called, "Domino Theory & Strategy", and volunteers through his church to teach his afterschool program, "Dominoes, More Than A Game," in elementary schools.

Travis and Maryalice currently reside in a Chicago suburb near their children and granddaughters.

Travis can be contacted at travisnewsome@travisnewsome.com

Edward J. Newsome

Biography

Edward J. Newsome was born in the cotton fields in Chappell Hill, Texas, where he learned the value of hard work and the meaning of strong family dynamics. He is the 5th of eleven children. Edward is a born-again believer and has dedicated his life to the service of others. He holds a Bachelor of Arts degree in political science from the University of Missouri-Kansas City and a Juris Doctorate degree from the University of Missouri-Kansas City School of Law.

Answering the call to serve his country, he had a dynamic two-year stint in the U.S. Army serving as a combat paratrooper in Vietnam, where he was involved in more than 50 combat assaults. In addition to being awarded the Bronze Star for valor, he earned 10 other combat related medals. In the past 8 years he has traveled to northern Ethiopia 12 times as a part-time missionary where he founded the Matthew 25 Children's Project of Ethiopia, an organization that has helped to find the sponsors needed for 52 children and their families.

Over the years, he has served on the National Down Syndrome Congress Board, the Missouri Planning Council for Developmental Disabilities, and the Jackson County Board of Services for Developmental Disabilities. He was also elected to the Kansas City Board of Education, where he served two years as the president of the board.

Edward is a founding member of the United Believers Community Church (Kansas City) and serves as chairman of the deacon's ministry. He is married to Cynthia Gunn-Newsome, former anchor at KSHB television station. Edward was formerly married to Patricia Hill Newsome. He and Patricia have two adult children, Edward II and Kimberly. Kimberly was adopted at birth.

Edward's favorite pastimes are playing dominoes and doing puzzles. He is currently writing a book for his son with Down Syndrome about the tremendous impact fathers can have on their children by getting an early start with identifying and establishing the necessary support in the life of a child with Down Syndrome.

Edward can be contacted at
ejnewsome@gmail.com

Delores Newsome-French

Biography

Delores Newsome French is the tenth child born to John Douglas Newsome and Ina Turknett Newsome in Chappell Hill, Texas on August 20th, 1956.

Her life growing up in Chappell Hill basically consisted of going to school and attending church, and besides that, there was little or no social life.

She attended a segregated elementary school in Chappell Hill where she enjoyed and excelled in school, skipped the fifth grade and graduated the sixth grade as salutatorian. She and her parents opted for her to attend an integrated middle school and an integrated high school in Brenham, Texas where she and other children in the community had to be bussed the ten miles. After high school, and prior to her seventeenth birthday, Delores moved to Kansas City, Missouri.

Prior to her 21st birthday, Delores gave birth to her first child, Jayneice. As a single mother, she worked part-time, and with family support, was able to eventually complete her education, obtaining a Bachelor of Science in electrical engineering at the University of Missouri - Kansas City in 1983. After working a few years in telecommunications, she continued working full-time and went back to school part-time and obtained a Master of Business Administration from

Baker University in 1994. Delores worked in telecommunications for 33 years and retired in December of 2016. After retirement, she worked for 1 ½ years as a high school business teacher.

Delores is a wife (married to Jeffrey French), mother (of Jayneice and Julian), grandmother (of Desmond, Jr., Bria & Brooke) and great-grandmother (of Adonis), all of whom live in the Kansas City metropolitan area.

Delores has always regarded education as a priority and has tried to emphasize its importance to her children and grandchildren, as a means towards independence. Since her retirement, Delores has served in the non-profit sector with Awesome Ambitions and also Days for Girls. Awesome Ambitions helps to mentor young women to have success through higher education and career planning. Days for Girls focuses on shattering stigmas and limitations associated with menstruation for improved health, education and livelihood outcomes for girls and women around the world. She enjoys traveling, playing dominoes, cooking, and hanging out with family and friends.

Johnnie Mae Newsome-Lewis

Biography

Johnnie Mae Newsome-Lewis was born on October 18th, 1940. She is the second oldest of 11 children born to the late J.D. Newsome and Ina Turknett Newsome in Washington County, Chappell Hill, Texas. She is a widow with two daughters, five grandchildren and two great grandchildren.

She grew up in the small town of Chappell Hill, Texas where she attended public school. She graduated from C.H. Hogan Junior High School (the 10th grade) in 1958, as the salutatorian of her class. In September she continued her education by attending Pickard High School in Brenham, Texas. Johnnie excelled in many areas of her studies, one of which was receiving an award for being the best mathematician in chemistry. She graduated in May of 1960 as the valedictorian of her class.

In June of 1960, Johnnie moved to Houston, Texas to live with Maurine Wilburn (her dad's cousin) and Maurine's husband, Ervin Wilburn. -After Johnnie graduated from high school, she received a $100 scholarship. She had plans to attend Texas Southern University in the fall, after working during the summer to help with tuition, but those plans did not materialize.

Johnnie later moved out on her own. She had several jobs throughout the years. She went to the University of Houston Real Estate School and practiced real estate for a short while. She was also part owner of a Freight Delivery Service.

Later in life, Johnnie decided to make a career change. She attended Houston Community College, where she majored in nursing. She had perfect attendance and also made the Dean's list. After finishing school, she became a nurse where she loved and devoted a lot of time helping the sick.

After retiring from nursing, she continued, and enjoyed helping others. Her passion is cooking, and she loves cooking for and feeding others. Johnnie also spent time traveling for pleasure, and at times to help sick family members, assisting in every way possible.